Rethink it!

Practical ways to rid yourself of anger, depression, jealousy and other common problems

By

Michael Cohen

Rethink it!

Practical ways to rid yourself of anger, depression, jealousy and other common problems

By

Michael Cohen

Bookline & Thinker Ltd

Bookline & Thinker Ltd
#231, 405 King's Road
London SW10 0BB
Tel: 0845 116 1476
www.booklinethinker.com

The right of Michael Cohen to be identified as the author of this
work has been asserted in accordance with the Copyright, Designs
and Patents Act 1988.

The author's moral rights have been asserted.

A CIP catalogue for this book is available from the British Library.

ISBN: 9780993287404

Cover design by Gee Mac
Printed and bound by Lightning Source UK

Important Notice

This book is designed to provide information in regard to the subject matter covered. It is not intended to be a substitute for medical or psychological advice or treatment. It is sold with the understanding that the publisher and author are not engaged in rendering psychological, financial, legal or other services. Any person with a condition requiring medical or psychological attention should consult a qualified medical practitioner or suitable therapist.

All client names and cases mentioned have been disguised to protect their privacy and confidentiality.

Dedication

To my dear parents Loretta and Gerald

Contents

Rethink it!

Part 1 - Be your own best friend

1. What do you say when you talk to yourself?	1
2. Don't get derailed by distorted thinking	5
3. How demands lead to misery	17
4. Overcoming feelings of shame and embarrassment	22
5. Unconditionally accepting yourself and others	28
6. Overcoming worry	33

Part 2 - Relax and Heal Negative Emotions

7. Anxiety	45
8. Depression	60
9. Anger	68
10. Jealousy	74
11. Relax, breathe and stay sane	79

Part 3 - Change your behaviour

12. How to stop smoking	88
13. Weight loss – the psychological strategies that work	95
14. How to be assertive	101
15. It's good to talk	110
16. Relationship matters	116
17. Overcoming blushing	122

Part 1

Be your own best friend

What do you say when you talk to yourself?

You have heard the statement: *"Talking to yourself is the first sign of madness."* We talk to ourselves most of the time, even though we may not realise it. This self-talk takes place internally within the privacy of our own mind. All too often, self-talk is harsh, self-defeating, counterproductive and even abusive. We give ourselves labels that can prevent us from experiencing a truly happy, productive and fulfilling life. If you've developed a negative style of talking to yourself, you may be missing opportunities, performing below your potential and experiencing more stress than necessary.

In a similar way to negative comments from other people, our own internal dialogue can have a dramatic effect on how we feel, especially when it consists of unkind and unhelpful language.

Sometimes, this negative self-talk has a personal or historical root. It is as children that we first internalise unhelpful ideas. Parents, teachers, religious figures and others can lead us to believe negative and unjustified ideas about ourselves. If we are continually in an environment

1

where we are being judged or criticised, our own internal dialogue takes on an extremely negative tone.

So that...

"You're stupid," becomes *"I'm stupid."*

"You're bad," becomes *"I'm bad."*

"You're selfish," becomes *"I'm selfish."*

"That's far too difficult for you – don't even try," becomes *"Why bother,"* and so on.

Since the things we say to ourselves can have such a powerful effect on the way we feel and act, negative self-talk often leads to fear, anxiety and depression. Harmful self-talk can be triggered by all sorts of events, including social and work-related situations, and can occur when both good and bad things happen.

Fortunately, the reverse is also true. You can turn negative self-talk into an optimistic, positive-style of thinking. Martin Seligman, an American professor of psychology, has studied the way people explain the positive and negative events in their lives. His research shows that pessimists tend to base their view of the world on negative events. Conversely, optimists tend to distance themselves from negative events and gravitate towards the positive.

As an example, imagine that you are at a friend's home and you drop a mug of coffee. Do you see this as a small accident that occurred because you were distracted, or do you feel ashamed and tell yourself you're an awkward fool? If you're a pessimist, you're likely to label yourself as the awkward fool, whereas optimists are far more likely to accept it as an accident.

Replacing negative self-talk with a positive attitude will create good feelings and set you on the path to achieving healthy emotions.

Rethink it!

Instead of:

"I will never succeed with this project – it's hopeless and so am I."

Say:

"I have achieved more than I am giving myself credit for. I am not hopeless and have a very good chance of succeeding."

Instead of:

"She thinks I'm attractive – she must be mad!"

Say:

"I'm going to ask her out on a date – I hope she'll say yes."

Instead of:

"My presentation is going to be terrible! I'll be the laughing stock of the office."

Say:

"I have given successful presentations before. This one is likely to be well received."

Other ways to challenge negative self-talk:

What would you say to a best friend?

3

Your best friend comes to you for support. She's in tears because she's made a mistake and is berating herself mercilessly.

Do you say?

"I agree with you. You have made a terrible mistake that you can never put right. You, of all people, should really know better. You are a horrible person who should be thoroughly ashamed of yourself."

Perhaps a family member comes to you because he or she is discouraged and on the verge of giving up on an important project.

Would you say?

"Yes, give up now. In fact, you should have given up months ago. You know you're weak – a loser who's destined to never amount to anything. It's only going to get harder, so why try? What were you thinking anyway?"

I'm sure your answer to both of these is a resounding NO! The reality is that you would want to show your friend empathy in a positive and reassuring manner. After all, a friend is meant to be someone who believes in you when you have given up believing in yourself.

But wait...do you talk to yourself in ways you would never contemplate when talking to a friend or family member?

In times of need, do you offer comfort and support to your friends and loved ones, but reprimand yourself with harsh and critical putdowns?

4

If so, why the double standard?

Remember, be your own best friend. Whatever encouraging words you'd say to your best friend, say those words to yourself. You deserve it.

Keep a diary of your negative thoughts

Whenever you experience a negative thought, write it down in a diary and explain what triggered it. Review your diary on a regular basis. Was your negativity truly justified? Is there another way to view the situation? For example, change:

"I'm an idiot for losing my job. I will never find another one like it."

To:

"It's unfortunate that I lost my job. I wish I had been more efficient. I don't like losing my job, but I can handle it. Finding another job may be challenging, but I can do it!"

Just by paying attention to how you talk to yourself, you can make huge changes in your life. Often, a negative inner dialogue has taken years to develop, so creating a positive one will take time as well. However, with work and practise, you can greatly boost your confidence.

Don't be derailed by distorted thinking

Distorted thoughts have a way of making our lives miserable. The errors in our thinking are known as cognitive

5

distortions and were first observed by the pioneering American psychiatrist Dr Aaron Beck back in the 1960s. Cognitive distortions are patterns of thought that lead people to perceive reality in a negative form. These unhelpful and distorted thinking patterns convince people that their interpretation of events are accurate and true, when in reality they are not.

Indeed, cognitive distortions generate inaccurate, exaggerated and generally self-defeating thought patterns that interfere with how a person interprets an event, usually leading to upsetting and destructive emotions. In other words, our mind convinces us of something that isn't really true. If you're suffering from distorted thinking, you're probably seeing yourself, others and the world around you in a negative light, which can lead to depression, anxiety and a whole range of emotional issues.

Although it was Beck who first developed the theory of cognitive distortion, it was his student, the noted psychiatrist and author Dr David Burns, who expanded and popularised the concept. In his best-selling 1980 book, *Feeling Good – The New Mood Therapy*, Burns gave names to the following 11 cognitive distortions:

1. All or nothing thinking

Also referred to as black and white thinking, all or nothing thinking occurs when a person's thoughts fall into good or bad categories, without leaving any room for middle ground.

For example:

Sarah is determined to stop smoking and sets a date to quit. The day arrives, and within six hours, she has a puff of a cigarette. Despite immediately extinguishing it and throwing the remaining cigarettes away, Sarah says to herself: *"That's it … I have failed to stop completely."*

This thought upsets Sarah so much that she purchases another pack of cigarettes and smokes them all that day.

Rethink it!

I asked Sarah to challenge herself and think of times when she had stopped smoking, even if only for a few days or hours. Instead of viewing her most-recent attempt to quit as a complete failure, I suggested she think of what happened as a mistake, and remind herself that she can choose to get back on track with her smoking cessation plans. Remember, there are few situations that are absolute.

Whenever Sarah finds herself faced with a similar quandary, she now asks herself:

"Is it really so bad, or am I indulging in all or nothing thinking?"

"How else can I think about the situation?"

"Am I taking a balanced view or thinking in an extreme way?"

2. Overgeneralisation

An overgeneralisation occurs when a person comes to a general conclusion based on a single incident or a single piece of evidence. If something bad happens just once, the person expects it to happen over and over again, seeing a single, unpleasant event as part of a never-ending pattern of defeat. He may use words such as "always" and "never" when thinking about it, and assumes it will automatically happen again.

"I always miss my train."

"I never get anything right."

"Nothing works out for me."

Example:

James arranges a picnic for his family in late August. Although the weather forecast suggests it will be dry and sunny, it rains for most of the time and the family ends up getting drenched.

James says to himself: *"Typical! It always rains when I arrange an outdoor outing for the family."*

Rethink it!

I asked James if his statement that it always rains when he arranges outdoor events for his family is 100 per cent true. After a short pause, he smiled and mentioned that his family enjoyed a very pleasant day out on Brighton beach earlier in the year. Now, when James is tempted to overgeneralise, he asks himself:

"Am I over-generalising?"

"What are the facts?"

"Are my interpretations accurate?"

3. Mental filter

A mental filter occurs when we take the negative details of a situation or event and magnify them while filtering out all the positive aspects. For instance, a person may pick out a single, unpleasant detail about an experience and dwell on it exclusively until their version of reality becomes overly negative or distorted.

Example: Nicky is asked to speak at a colleague's leaving party. Afterwards, 19 out of 20 people say nice things about the speech. However, one person makes a mildly critical remark. Nicky obsesses about the comment for hours while ignoring all the positive feedback.

Rethink it!

I asked Nicky if she realised she was zeroing in on the one negative comment and dismissing all the compliments. Immediately, she could see that she was being hard on herself. In future, Nicky has decided to ask herself:

"Am I looking at the negatives, while ignoring the positives?"

"Is there a more balanced way to view this situation?"

4. Discounting the positive

Discounting the positive involves ignoring or invalidating good things that have happened. People who discount the positive often overlook their achievements while being quick to notice their faults. They discount their success, believing it was just luck or chance. People who discount the positive rarely feel any sense of pride or satisfaction in their achievements.

Example:

Tim wins salesperson of the year and is awarded a cheque for £2,000 and a plaque as acknowledgement of his exceptional performance. Tim feels very uncomfortable with this award and refuses to take up the offer of a drink with his co-workers. He discounts the recognition, saying he was just doing his job and hadn't done anything out of the ordinary to deserve it. Tim puts his plaque in a drawer and never mentions it to anyone outside of work.

Rethink it!

Tim's lack of self-worth kept him from enjoying his award. Instead of minimising his recognition, I encouraged Tim to express gratitude for it. I suggested he think about why the company had awarded him a £2,000 cheque. Tim began to reconsider his stance and realised that he did do a lot of extra work and deserved the award. Now Tim:

Examines evidence for and against discounting positives.

Asks himself if everyone would see it this way... if not, why not?

He reminds himself that if everyone thought so negatively of him, there would be different consequences.

5. Mind reading

An individual who is mind reading makes a negative interpretation about what others are thinking, even though there is no evidence to support this conclusion. Despite nothing being said, mind readers believe they know what people think and feel about them, as well as why they behave the way they do towards them.

Example:

Jenny is at a party and due to anxiety is finding it hard to make conversation. She decides: *"Everyone is looking down their nose at me … the people I have managed to speak to must think I'm really stupid."*

Rethink it!

I ask Jenny if she has any real evidence that anyone – let alone everyone – is looking down on her. Did she think that maybe she was being too hard on herself? Jenny realised that she was mind reading and asked herself the following.

"What is the evidence that people are looking down their nose at me?"

"How do I know what other people are thinking?"

"Just because I assume something, does that mean I'm right?"

"What else could they be thinking that is positive?"

6. Fortune telling

Fortune telling involves anticipating the worst and taking it as fact. When a person is fortune telling, he believes he knows what the future holds. He makes negative predictions and is convinced they are unavoidable facts.

Example:

Peter is on his way to a job interview and tells himself: *"I just know I'm going to be asked questions I cannot answer. It's all going to go horribly wrong."*

Rethink it!

I ask Peter: *"Have you ever predicted disaster about a job interview before, only to find it went far better than you expected?"* Peter's answer was a resounding, *"Yes."* Now he asks himself:

"Am I predicting disaster without evidence to back it up?"

7. Magnification

This distortion involves magnifying problems by blowing their effects way out of proportion. When things go wrong, we all have a tendency to exaggerate the consequences and imagine a disastrous outcome.

Example:

Frankie says to herself: *"This is the worst thing that could happen. It's awful and I can't cope!"*

Rethink it!

I ask Frankie:

"Realistically, what's the worst that could happen?"

"If the worst did happen, what would you do to cope?"

"What's most likely to happen?"

"In reality, is it really that awful or terrible?"

By answering these questions, Frankie was able to put the situation into perspective and reduce her anxiety.

8. Emotional reasoning

Emotional reasoning is a negative style of thinking in which people base their view of themselves, other people, or a situation on the way they feel, rather than taking reality into account. A person assumes that his feelings reflect fact, regardless of the evidence. He assumes that what he feels must be true.

"I feel like a failure, so I must be one."

"I wouldn't be worrying if there wasn't something to worry about."

"I feel unattractive, so I must be."

Example:

James is anxious about air travel, so he reasons that flying on a modern aircraft is a risky and dangerous thing to do. Because James' reasoning is based on emotion, he doesn't stop to consider the facts.

Rethink it!

I asked James to consider that he might be confusing his feelings with the facts, and pointed out that if flying really was that dangerous, then why doesn't everyone who boards an aircraft feel anxious? James could see he was confusing his thoughts and feelings with reality. Now he asks himself:

"Am I confusing my feelings with the facts?"

"Do my feelings necessarily reflect reality?"

"Am I thinking this way just because I'm feeling bad right now?"

9. Shoulds and musts

"I SHOULD be a better person."

"People MUST treat me in a fair, polite way."

"The world MUST always be the way I want it to be."

These kinds of statements are called irrational beliefs. They are demands we place on ourselves, others and the world. Our demands can lie at the very core of our difficulties, leading to depression, anger and a "why bother?" attitude. Our aim is to replace demands with preferences – to restructure our irrational unhealthy thinking with rational healthy alternative thoughts. Since this is such an important form of distorted thinking, I have devoted a whole segment to it, *How demands lead to misery.*

10. Labelling

Labelling is an extreme type of all or nothing thinking, as well as an overgeneralisation. Instead of describing a specific behaviour, a person assigns a negative or self-defeating label to himself or others.

Example:

Michael had spent a whole weekend writing an article for an in-house magazine. On Monday morning, his computer hard drive failed. To make matters worse, Michael had failed to back up his article onto an external drive. Michael said to himself: *"I'm a complete loser."*

Rethink it!

I asked Michael what good could possibly come from calling himself names. Instead, I suggested he be specific and judge his actions, rather than himself. For example, noting that it was a stupid thing to do is a far better response than putting himself down, which would only make him feel worse. After re-evaluating the situation, Michael came to a more specific conclusion:

"Not backing up my work was a stupid error. I made a mistake after a busy week."

11. Personalisation and blame

Personalisation and blame occur when someone automatically assumes responsibility for negative events that are not under their control. Sometimes, people will blame others for their circumstances while overlooking how they may have contributed to the problem.

Example:

Sarah took her two children and their two friends to see a film they had all been looking forward to. Not one of the children enjoyed the film, so Sarah ended up blaming herself.

Rethink it!

I asked Sarah if she was being reasonable by blaming herself for the children's lack of enjoyment. Realising that she couldn't be expected to take responsibility, she now asks herself:

"Am I really to blame for other people's actions and emotions?"

"Is this really all about me?"

When you're feeling down, focus on your thinking. If your thoughts are negative or critical, look for the thinking errors and challenge them. Once you get into the habit of disputing your negative self-talk, you'll find it easier to handle difficult situations. As a result, you'll feel less stressed, more confident and in control.

How demands lead to misery

Did you know that our feelings and behaviour are largely dependent on the way we think about the events in our lives? In order to lead a psychologically healthy life, it is important that we hold beliefs that enable us to develop a positive attitude towards ourselves, others and the world at large. If we hold rigid, dogmatic and unhelpful beliefs, then we are likely to experience unhealthy emotions and psychological distress. On the other hand, if our beliefs and attitudes are flexible, we are likely to exhibit healthy emotions and behaviours that allow us to achieve our goals and live a happy life.

Three major demands that lead to emotional misery:

We all desire good things to happen to us, and want to avoid bad things. However, we also have a strong tendency to elevate these desires into absolute demands. When we hold onto demanding and dogmatic beliefs, we become upset. It is this rigidity that lies at the core of our emotionally disturbed responses to negative events.

According to the pioneering American psychologist Dr Albert Ellis, irrational beliefs are central to emotional distress. Dr Ellis identified three major demands that create this distress. Often referred to as the three 'major musts', they are:

Demands we place on ourselves - such as: *"I must do well or else I'm no good."*

Demands we place on others

Such as: *"People must treat me fairly and kindly, and if they don't, they are no good."*

Demands we place on the world

Such as: *"Life must go the way I want, when I want."*

"The universe must treat me well."

These demands lead to emotional misery. The first can trigger anxiety, depression, guilt and shame. The second is behind a great deal of anger, aggression and even acts of violence. The third can cause self-pity, depression and a "why bother?" attitude.

Let's look a little closer at these three demands:

1. Demands we place on ourselves

It is natural, healthy and good to want to achieve success in all that we do in life. But problems can arise when we place unduly high expectations on ourselves and elevate a desire to do well into an absolute demand that we MUST do well. Then, if we aren't as successful as we'd demanded, we exaggerate the severity of the situation and run ourselves down. We tell ourselves that the situation is hopeless and that we are failures and no good. This can then lead to self-denigration and even self-hatred.

2. Demands we place on others

It is perfectly reasonable to want people to treat us with respect, and to be polite and courteous. However, as with the first demand, problems can arise when we elevate the desire to be treated well into an absolute insistence that we MUST be treated well all the time. Then, when people fail to live up to our expectations, we feel aggrieved and condemn them, which can lead to rage and anger.

3 Demands we place on the world

Do you demand that life must be easy, without discomfort or inconvenience? It is reasonable to desire that the world be a safe place and to prefer that things go the way that we want them to go. However, problems arise when we become inflexible and insist that circumstances must turn out the way we want. This can make tolerating frustration difficult and result in self-pity, anxiety and depression.

"Shoulds" and "Musts"

In common everyday language, everybody uses words such as "should" and "must."

"I really should get to my hospital appointment on time."

"I must wait for the pedestrian lights to turn green before I cross the road."

The above statements can be very helpful and potentially life saving. However, "should", "must", "have to" and "got to" can become unhelpful when used in the context of an unreasonable demand. If you insist that you must or should have things such as success, fairness and convenience, you are demanding that the world dances to your tune and that your rules are always obeyed. Demands could include:

"People must treat me fairly all the time."

"The world should always be a fair place."

Example:

Deborah was feeling anxious about a presentation she had to give to a group of associates at work. Deborah tells herself: *"I must give a perfect presentation or I've failed."*

You can now see how these irrational beliefs can leave a person feeling anxious. As we have seen, demands consist of irrational beliefs. They are unrealistic, rigid, blow events way out of proportion and are inconsistent with reality. They lead to unhealthy feelings that can cause misery and distress. On the other hand, preferences consist of rational beliefs and are realistic, flexible and aligned with reality. They keep events in perspective and lead to healthy, appropriate feelings.

Preferences contain statements such as:

"I would like to, but I don't have to."

"I prefer to, but I don't have to."

"I hope to, but there are no guarantees."

Rethink it!

I indicated to Deborah that rather than holding onto

counter-productive demands, she would be better off thinking in terms of preferences. I suggested that a more flexible attitude would reduce her anxiety, and that she should dispute the idea that her presentation must be perfect. Deborah challenged her irrational beliefs by asking herself:

"Why must I give a perfect presentation?"

"I really would like to give a perfect presentation, but does it follow that I have to?"

"How would giving a less than perfect presentation make me less successful?"

After challenging her "shoulds" and "musts", Deborah arrived at the far more flexible belief:

"I would prefer to give a perfect presentation, but it's not absolutely necessary."

This reduced her anxiety considerably, allowing her to enjoy giving an outstanding, but not completely perfect, presentation.

It is important to recognise that you have far more control over your thoughts and feelings than you realise. Other people can physically punch you in the stomach, causing you physical pain. They may also be able to frustrate your plans and cause mischief. However, it is you and only you who largely creates your emotional suffering and self-defeating behaviour. It can be liberating to recognise that you have a choice as to how you think, feel and respond to upsetting events in your life. When under pressure, most people have trouble thinking rationally. You have probably been thinking in irrational ways for a long time. However, by putting in the effort to challenge and change your thoughts, you will soon find yourself getting less upset.

Overcoming feelings of shame and embarrassment

Many people feel shame and embarrassment because they are worried about what others may think of them. Those who say they never worry about this are probably being economical with the truth because this particular worry trait is something we've inherited from our ancestors.

Many years ago, we all lived in small hunter-gatherer tribes where everyone knew each other and built their lives together. Of utmost importance was survival and attracting the best mate in order to pass on our genes. Within the tribe, status and authority were key ingredients, so fitting in and being liked was essential. Say or do the wrong thing and we risked being excluded from the group. Abandoned and alone, we would be left to fend for ourselves in a dangerous, hostile world. Being obsessively worried about doing and saying the right thing was appropriate then, but is that still the case in today's world?

These days, we can decide which tribe is ours. We also have far more choice about our role within that group.

Make a mistake or say something inappropriate, and we are far more likely to be forgiven. Even if we do become ostracised from one set of friends, it's unlikely to affect our standing within other groups.

Our modern world also gives us far more opportunity and freedom to choose potential mates than the ancient world ever did – something our ancestors could only dream about. So when we fear looking foolish, worry about what others think or find ourselves obsessing about a work presentation, we are in part buying into an ancient ancestral trait.

If talking to strangers, asking someone out on a date or discussing issues with your boss leads to a significant anxious feeling in the pit of your stomach, it could be that your emotional reaction is keeping you from experiencing pleasure and satisfaction, acting assertively or sharing intimacy in your life. People who feel shame and embarrassment often rate themselves in a very negative light. They may condemn themselves, and put themselves down. Yet most of the behaviours we feel ashamed about amount only to things we would prefer not to have done. For example, we may bring some unnecessary attention to ourselves by doing something perceived as stupid, but does that make us a stupid person?

It may be helpful to regret having done certain things, but to berate yourself and be filled with self-criticism is potentially damaging and certainly self-defeating. Why feel ashamed and blow out of proportion something that others would merely regret? Is it truly the end of the world if something we say comes out the wrong way? Even if people do laugh at you or form a negative impression, so what? They're judging you on one short meeting and don't know who you truly are. Little purpose is served in the modern world by shame and embarrassment, and these painful feelings could be preventing you from experiencing self-worth, hope for the future, friendship and love.

Rethink it!

Here are some ideas to help you stop worrying about what other people think of you.

1. Remember those ancestral traits

People are normally too hung up worrying about what others think about them to have time to think about you. Attempting to read someone's mind doesn't work, and can lead to catastrophic thinking. Even if someone's laughing, it doesn't automatically mean she thinks less of you as a person, and it isn't necessarily directed at you. While you're busy thinking about whether you came across as you'd hoped, the other person has moved on!

2. What other people think of you is none of your business

Spending time worrying about what others think serves no purpose. Needily seeking the approval of others is a waste of your time and emotional energy. What is important is not whether others approve of you, but whether you approve of yourself. Instead of worrying about how those you meet choose to perceive you, focus on fulfilling your own potential. How people see you is governed by their own interpretations, and shaped by their personal beliefs and judgments – therefore it's none of your business.

3. You don't need other people's approval to be happy

Don't wait for other people's permission before living the life you want to lead. Your confidence and sense of self-worth do not depend on whether they approve of your decisions. While you may prefer to acknowledge the opinions of those close to you, don't allow what they think to prevent you from leading a life that makes you happy. Besides, you can never really know what other people are thinking. Just because you are carrying around shameful or embarrassed feelings doesn't mean everyone else is judging you and, even if they are, you don't have to take their opinions seriously.

4. You can overcome shame by attacking it head on.

One of the most effective ways of overcoming shame and embarrassment is through the use of a shame-attacking exercise. This concept was developed by the noted psychologist and founder of rational emotive behaviour therapy, Albert Ellis. To help his clients overcome fear, shame and embarrassment, Dr Ellis would prescribe an exercise that forced them to challenge their feelings.

The best way to deal with fear and uncertainty, in Dr Ellis' opinion, is to focus on the worst-case scenario rather than the best-case scenario.

To overcome the fear of shame, you might be asked to deliberately act in a shameful way in order to attract criticism and disapproval from other people. By doing so, you prove to yourself that even if you do look silly and are criticised, it's not the end of the world and you can tolerate other people's judgements, even if you do feel highly uncomfortable.

By practising shame attacking, you learn that:

1. You can accept yourself and not put yourself down even when you do foolish things.

2. That you probably overestimate the negative reactions of other people to your behaviour, even when you consider it shameful.

3. That while it is preferable not to behave in a stupid way, it isn't the end of the world if you do.

4. That you can cope even when people give you disapproving looks or criticise you for your behaviour.

Important note: Shame-attacking exercises should not put you or others at risk of harm and should not involve breaking the law. Please be sensible and don't do anything that is likely to have a negative consequence, such as the loss of your job or damage to a relationship.

Examples of shame-attacking exercises:

Go into a department store lift and announce in a loud voice the floor number and what items are sold on that floor.

Wear a sweater or shirt inside-out or back-to-front in public.

Walk into a newsagent and announce you've been time-travelling and don't know what year it is.

During my training as a therapist, I practised the last example during a lunch break and got some very strange looks. However, even though I felt a build-up of anxiety as I approached the newsagent, I quickly discovered that nothing terrible happened as a consequence. Indeed, it gave the customers a rather amusing shopping experience.

When you practise a shame-attacking exercise, your head is very likely to be filled with negative shameful beliefs. It is important to vigorously dispute these.

For instance, with my newsagent experience I told myself that:

"Just because I acted in a foolish manor, it doesn't mean I am a foolish person."

Rational beliefs can help to cancel out the irrational beliefs. When you practise shame attacking, you will discover that, more often than not, hardly anyone pays any attention or cares when you act in an eccentric way. If someone does notice, discovering that you can cope is a great relief.

Unconditionally accept yourself and others

Do you believe that your worth depends on what you achieve in life? Do you measure your value based on how wealthy or popular you are? Or perhaps you base your acceptability as a person on how others judge you. If you fail to achieve, do you think of yourself as a worthless individual?

Society influences us from an early age to base our worth on our accomplishments. We deal with unrealistic expectations assigned to us by the demanding society in which we live. So-called 'winners' are worshipped while others are labelled as 'losers' and forgotten. Society so often tells us that what we do is important, but what we are is not.

By using achievements such as work advancement and how much you are liked by significant people to measure your self-worth, you risk sliding into depression or anxiety if you fail to accomplish an objective or live up to other people's expectations of you.

Is self-esteem the answer?

Society, self-help books and pop psychologists all tell us that, in order to thrive and be happy, we need high self-esteem. But this poses the question: does self-esteem help us to foster an unconditional self-accepting attitude towards ourselves and others?

To esteem yourself means to rate yourself. A person's self-esteem will seem to be high when they are performing well and feeling competent. However, it is all too easy for self-esteem to plummet when a person falls short of a goal, is rejected by a potential partner or feels unworthy when not living up to expectations. This is how self-esteem becomes conditional and brief, leading people to feel good one minute while condemning themselves the next.

For example, when you achieve success, you may think to yourself: *"I am a good person"*; then when you face a setback, you say: *"I failed and am therefore a bad person."*

We also base self-esteem on how others react to us. So when you win the approval of significant people in your life, your self-esteem is high, and when they reject you, it is low.

It is natural to feel good when you perform well. Let us suppose that a singer gives an excellent performance at a concert. She gets a standing ovation with many compliments and excellent reviews in the press. The singer feels really good about herself and her ability to perform in such a powerful way. She has been singing professionally for a number of years. The better she performs, the better she feels and the higher her self-esteem becomes.

The problem with this approach is that our singer will eventually run into trouble because everyone, including the exceptionally gifted, fails to perform well some of the time.

As the legendary psychologist Albert Ellis noted: *"When you succeed in getting what you want, you say, 'that is good. Great!' But you also rate yourself and say, 'I am a good person for succeeding!' When you fail to achieve your goals, you say, 'that is bad and I am bad.'"*

According to Ellis, self-esteem is probably the greatest emotional disturbance known to the human race.

So if you make your worth as a person depend on your achievements, your feelings of self-worth will be temporary. Measuring your self-worth in this way will frequently lead to depression and self-loathing whenever you fail to live up to your goals.

The singer feels good because she receives a standing ovation from the audience along with great press reviews. Winning the approval of others can be seen as a good thing – nothing wrong with that. But the problem arises when the singer concludes that because the audience and reviewers think highly of her performance that makes her a good and worthy person. She ties up her worth as a person with her ability to sing and perform well, as well as with the opinions of others.

The following week, our singer gives another performance that fails to impress. This time, there is a lacklustre response from the audience. The press are very critical, stating that her poor performance reveals she is losing her touch. The singer's feelings of self-worth plummet. Before even taking the time to think about her circumstances and why her recital wasn't so good this time, she concludes that, because it was inadequate, she is inadequate. Our singer confuses a below par performance with being a lesser person.

Other examples of this confusion include equating making a mistake with being a mistake; having a failure with being a failure; and doing something that is bad with being a bad person.

This denigration of the self is wrong and a prescription for further failure. If people define themselves as a total failure then they minimise their chances of success in the future. The singer told herself that she was "inadequate as a person" for giving a performance that wasn't up to her usual standard. But how could an inadequate person have given previous performances that were considered excellent?

The more people put themselves down, the less likely they are to perform well because they are quite literally prescribing failure for themselves.

From the above example, we can see that self-esteem can be a ratings game. You rate yourself, your essence, even your whole being. This may appear to work when life is going well; you have a good career, satisfying relationships and enough money. However, problems arise when you tell yourself you're a good person for having these things, because – as you have no doubt experienced – things don't always go so well. Something may go wrong, you may feel rejected by a significant person or lose some money; then your feelings of self-worth may well plummet. The mistake you make is to tie your self-worth up with your success and achievements; and being fallible, like all people, there will be times when you fail.

Unconditional self-acceptance

There is an antidote to this dilemma, which, surprisingly, is rooted in ancient history. Centuries ago, Greek and Roman philosophers developed the concept of self-acceptance. They saw that in order for a person to be fully self-accepting, it was vital to never rate yourself or other people. The psychologist Dr Albert Ellis has termed this *'unconditional self-acceptance.'*

Suppose you receive the gift of a bouquet of flowers, but discover that one of the flowers is mouldy and dead. Do you recoil in horror and throw the whole bunch of flowers into the bin, or do you remove the dead flower and arrange the rest into a nice vase? Of course, the majority of us would make the latter sensible choice and enjoy the bouquet. However, do we do the same when it comes to ourselves, or do we tend to condemn both the rotten things we do – our mistakes and failures – and our whole selves, our very essence? To regret negative things we do can be helpful, especially if we then go on to put things right. But to condemn not only what we do, but who we are, leads to anxiety, guilt, insecurity, jealousy, depression and anger.

When you refuse to rate yourself, you avoid these unhealthy emotions. By recognising that everyone has shortcomings and that nobody is perfect, you're in a better position to accept your weaknesses along with your strengths. It is healthy to rate your performance, and if you can change something or improve it, then so much the better. But if you cannot change it, then accept it and continue to do as well as you can.

Rethink it!

Practice unconditional self-acceptance

A. Think of situations in which you tend to judge your whole self. What could you say to yourself in these situations that would enable you to accept yourself unconditionally, regardless of any mistakes you may make or inadequacies you may possess?

B. Take 20 minutes a day separating yourself from your performances. It is vital that you do not judge yourself as either all good or all bad.

C. Apply unconditional acceptance to other people. Rate only their behaviours and traits as good or bad, but never rate them as a whole person.

Overcoming worry

Are you a chronic worrier constantly worrying your days away about almost everything? Do you worry about your health, work performance, being liked by others, your academic performance as well as a host of other issues? These worries can take a heavy toll, keeping you stressed and anxious during the day and wide awake at night. Worry eats away at you, causes you to feel tired and creates aches and pains; it can affect relationships, and even lead to depression.

Some people seem to have a predisposition to worrying about trivial matters before those worries have even seen the light of day, while others may only worry minimally about something once it has actually happened and then, if possible, go on to resolve it. Why is there this difference amongst people and what can be done about it?

Beliefs about worry

Samantha believes that her all-consuming worrying is harmful to her and that it is going to drive her insane. A year ago Samantha had a cancer scare which fortunately proved negative. However since that scare she worries about her health on a regular basis. She thinks worry is taking over her life and will cause her real physical ill-health. Family and friends have told her to pull herself together which causes her anger because she finds it so difficult to stop the worry.

Barry believes that his worrying serves a useful propose He thinks it keeps him alert and on guard helping him to avoid bad situations arising at work, prevent problems, and even helps him to resolve difficult situations.

It is self-evident that negative beliefs about worry create more worry and increase anxiety. Barry's positive belief about his worry can also take its toll and can be self-defeating – a problem rather than a solution.

What is worry?

According to Dr Robert Leahy, a leading expert in the field of cognitive therapy, worry is a strategy. If you are confronted with some worrying thoughts such as *"I might have a terminal disease"* or my *"boss might sack me,"* you activate a string of negative thoughts believing that if you worry excessively you may develop some form of control over events. You may also think that the worry will enable you to eliminate uncertainty and get an answer to the thing you are worrying about. So in this sense worry becomes your strategy. But has this approach ever truly worked for you? Is it productive? Has it ever given you the answer to your problems or has it just caused you more misery?

Jane was due to give a presentation to a group of associates at work. Jane would lie awake at night worrying about giving the presentation. She would say to herself:

"What if I can't remember what to say and go blank?"

"What will they say about me?"

"What if they think I'm stupid?"

"What if my presentation handouts don't make any sense?"

Jane's worrying thoughts are a demand for certainty.

What lies behind them is the demand that, *"I must be perfect and not make a mistake. If I do that would be terrible and people would think badly of me."*

While the last thing anyone wants is to make a mistake we all have to accept limitations.

We need to accept the possibility that we may make mistakes, that we never have complete control over events. We make mistakes because we are all fallible human beings.

Productive vs unproductive worry

Jane's first three thoughts are unproductive. There is very little she can do about them. However there is something she can do about the fourth thought. She can, for instance, check her notes for clarity, perhaps ask a colleague to read them to see if they can be improved upon or to scout for any spelling or grammatical mistakes. Therefore this thought is classified as a productive worry.

Make a list of your worries. Ask yourself:

Which of these worries is productive?

Which are unproductive?

Will these thoughts help me or hinder me?

Is there anything in these thoughts I can use today that will really help me make progress on the problem I am worrying about?

Then you can make a to-do list with the productive worries.

Rethink it!

Five Steps to End Chronic Worrying

Dr Robert Leahy has written extensively on the subject of worry and he has developed worry busting techniques:

1. "The Boredom Technique."

A technique that many people find helpful is to repeat a negative worry hundreds of times.

"What if I can't remember what to say and go blank?"

Repeating this thought for 15 to 20 minutes, slowly, and deliberately while focusing on the words will lead to you becoming incredibly bored with your worry. This is called, The Boredom Technique and can be very effective. By repeating a feared thought over and over again it will become boring, loose its power over you and will eventually go away.

2. Deliberately make yourself uncomfortable.

When we worry we tend to believe that we can't tolerate discomfort, but if you practice discomfort by putting yourself into the sort of situations that you worry about, you will accomplish control and worry a lot less. When we worry we tend to avoid new things and situations that make us uncomfortable, such as social situations or public speaking engagements. The initial 'what if' worries cause us to avoid discomfort, but if you force yourself to do the very things that make you uncomfortable, you will rely less on worry as a way of coping .

3. Create two daily worry times

Instead of resisting your worries, you choose periods during the day that you purposely devote to worrying. This is time you set aside exclusively for worry: an appointment with worry. This idea may seem odd because it runs counter to our usual instincts. But it's usually very helpful because, instead of "putting out fires with petrol," we are "fighting fire with fire."

The first worry time could be in the morning before you go off to work. Sit down in a place where you are unlikely to be disturbed and pay attention to your worries. Your second worry time could be right after you get home from work. This is how it is done:

A Set aside two daily 'Worry Times' of about 15 minutes each.

B Spend this time thinking only about your worries and only about one issue.

C Do not think about any positive alternatives but only the negative ones.

D Get yourself to become as anxious as you can while worrying.

E Reach the end of each worry time, even if you have run out of ideas and have to repeat the same worries over again.

F At the end of 15 minutes, let those worries go with some deep relaxing breaths, and return to your daily routine.

The main benefit of this technique comes about during the rest of your day, when you're not engaged in a worry period. If you find yourself worrying when you're not in your allotted worry period give yourself the following advice: I can either take 15 minutes now to worry very deliberately about this issue or postpone it to my next worry period.

The postponing can be very effective and enables many people to have large amounts of their day clear of worry. This technique involves a commitment; however the rewards can make it very worthwhile.

4. Challenge your worrying thoughts.

Do you treat every worry you have as a fact? Extreme worry can cause us to perceive situations as being far more dangerous than they actually are. We may for instance overestimate the possibility that things will go disastrously wrong, always imagining a worst case scenario while underestimating the possibility that they may not be nearly as bad as we imagine. We may also discount our ability to cope with challenging situations, forgetting that we have used our many resources to cope with difficult situations in the past. These unhelpful irrational attitudes are called cognitive distortions and you can read more about them in Part One Section 2. *Don't Get Derailed by Distorted Thinking.*

Challenging your worrying thoughts can help you to develop a more balanced view. Rather than viewing your thoughts as a forgone conclusion you test them out by challenging them. This is how it is done:

1. Identify and write down a situation you are worrying about – be specific.

2. Write down the worries you have about that situation.

3. Take each worrying thought in turn and challenge that thought by asking one or more of the following questions:

"What is the evidence that this thought is true?"

"What evidence do I have that what I am worrying about will actually happen?"

"What is the probability it will happen?"

"What are the more likely and realistic outcomes to this thing I am worrying about?"

"Is the thought helpful?"

"How will worrying about it help me?"

"How will worrying about it hurt me?"

"Is there a more positive, realistic way of looking at the situation?"

5. Relax your worries away.

Relaxation techniques such as mindfulness, deep breathing, and meditation can all help the worrier. In addition to the emotional factors involved, worrying can also bring on unpleasant physical sensations such as over breathing, tense painful muscles, headaches etc. Since you cannot be anxious and relaxed at the same time, strengthening your body's relaxation response makes a lot of sense as it can help reduce your worry.

In the next part of the book I expand on mindfulness and other relaxation techniques but in this section I will teach you a worry-busting relaxation technique called progressive muscle relaxation.

Progressive Muscle Relaxation

This technique focuses on deep muscle relaxation and was first developed in the 1920s by Dr Edmund Jacobson. Over the years it has been refined and modified so that it now involves tightening different muscle groups. If you have neck, back or teeth problems, you may wish to modify the procedure. If in doubt consult a qualified medic.

This is how it is done:

1. Sit or lie down in a quiet comfortable place. Remove contact lenses and any objects such as jewellery. Uncross your arms and legs. Take a deep breath and hold for as long as you find comfortable. Breath out – letting all feelings of tension leave your body.

2. Clench your right fist tight and then tighter. Notice the tension in your clenched fist, hand and arm. Now relax your fist and feel your right hand and arm go loose and limp. Notice the contrast with the tension. Repeat the procedure with your left fist and then both fists together.

3. Focus your attention on your forehead. Pull your eyebrows together as tightly as possible and hold. Now relax and let your forehead smooth out. Notice the contrast between tension and relaxation. Repeat the procedure and notice how relaxed your forehead becomes.

4. Close your eyes together as tightly as possible, feel the

tension. Now relax your eyes letting your eyelids droop. Keep your eyes closed, repeat the procedure. You can let your eyes remain closed for the rest of the exercise.

5. Clench your jaw biting your back teeth together. Feel the tension as it spreads throughout your jaw. Now relax your jaw. Once again, notice the contrast between tension and relaxation, then repeat the procedure.

6. Pull your head back as far as is comfortable. Feel the tension in your neck, hold, and then roll your head slowly to the right and then to the left. Notice the tension. Then straighten your head and bring it forward, pushing your chin onto your chest. Feel the tension in the back of your neck. Relax and allow your head to return to a comfortable position. Repeat the procedure and allow the relaxation to deepen.

7. Hunch your shoulders and hold for as long as is comfortable. Feel the tension. Then let your shoulders relax. Feel the relaxation spreading. Repeat the procedure and see how relaxed your shoulders can become.

8. Focus on the rhythm of your breathing, the rise and the fall of your diaphragm and chest. Notice how heavy your body is becoming with every breath that you take, feel your body relax just that little bit more.

9. Pull in your stomach muscles. Hold for as long as is comfortable, feel the tension and then relax. Repeat.

10. Tighten your buttocks and thighs. Push your heels down as hard as you can. Feel the tension, hold for as long

as is comfortable and then relax. Notice the contrast between the tension and relaxation. Repeat.

11. Point your toes in a downward direction and notice your calves growing tense. Feel the tension and hold for as long as is comfortable, then relax. Repeat.

12. Focus your attention on the comfortable feelings in your body, from the top of your head to the tips of your toes. Notice how relaxed you have become. You can now drift to a relaxing place in your imagination. It can be somewhere familiar to you or it may be an imaginary place that only exists in your mind. When you are ready, open your eyes.

For best results, practice progressive muscle relaxation on a regular basis for approximately 20 minutes each time. Do not rush it. After practicing the procedure you may notice tension in parts of your body that you thought did not exist. This is not an unusual experience and is an indication that you are becoming aware of the parts of your body where you hold onto tension. With practice this will pass.

Part 2
Relax and Heal Negative Emotions

Anxiety

Anxiety differs from normal feelings of nervousness. It is the body's natural response to danger – nature's alarm system that is triggered when a person feels under threat, is overwhelmed with pressure, or is facing a stressful situation. Of course, it's not unusual to feel some mild anxiety when facing a potentially stressful situation, such as a job interview, giving a presentation or asking for a pay rise. But if your thoughts and fears become overwhelming and interfere with your day-to-day life, you could be suffering from an anxiety disorder. If ignored, anxiety disorders can push people into avoiding situations that trigger or worsen their symptoms.

In some situations, we need to be alerted to impending danger. If you are in a building that is on fire or are confronted by a feral animal, you need a signal that warns you of the danger. Fortunately, nature has provided this and it is called the fight or flight response. When faced with a threat, the body reacts immediately with a rush of adrenaline, heightened muscle tension, faster heart rate and raised blood pressure. Blood pumps to the muscles and brain, causing the body to become alert and as strong as possible. This is because, in order to survive, a person needs to respond by either fighting the threat or running away from it.

Fight or flight is an appropriate response if your life is at risk due to a real emergency. However, we are rarely faced with life-threatening situations. Having to give a speech, travel by plane or ask a manager for a wage increase may be interpreted as unpleasant, but no-one's life is threatened. However, because, at some level, our minds consider the situation dangerous, an alarm is sent out triggering the fight or flight response. This can then lead us to believe we are in danger and trigger a host of symptoms, such as sweating, chest pains, feeling faint and a feeling of dread. This is often accompanied by catastrophic thinking, which further fuels the anxiety and panic.

Major types of anxiety

Anxiety is not as straightforward a condition as you may think and it can manifest in many different ways. The following are the major types of anxiety:

1. Generalised anxiety disorder

People with generalised anxiety disorder (GAD) have ongoing persistent feelings of nervousness that never seem to leave them. They may worry continually while feeling powerless to control their anxious mind. The worries can be about almost anything, from job issues, family concerns and health to getting to appointments or places on time. The anxiety can also manifest itself in more physical ways with persistent headaches, muscle pain and spasms, sleep disorders and eating issues. If your anxiety is constant then it's probably GAD.

Patrick's description of his GAD:

"I just seem to worry all the time, night and day. When I try to relax, I seem to become even more tense and that worries me. I cannot seem to get a good night's sleep. I wake up at least two or three times a night and sometimes find it hard to get back to sleep. I have regular headaches and backache. I feel like I will never get better."

2. Specific phobias

Fears are very common, but when a fear is irrational and so intense that it interferes with a person's day-to-day life, it is classed as a phobia. Many people have small phobias they can manage, and some fears are entirely appropriate. For instance, it is healthy to have a fear of crossing a busy road without looking left and right. Equally, I would worry if a person didn't have a fear of putting their naked hand in a fire. However, when the mere idea of, say, open spaces, spiders or getting in a lift causes stress and anxiety or otherwise affects a person's life, then it is time to do something about it.

Phobias can bring about catastrophic thinking. The sufferer will overestimate the risk to themselves while underestimating their ability to cope. Believing that the worst will happen, a phobic person may avoid certain situations. This is a mistake because avoidance will, in all likelihood, intensify the fear and prevent a person from developing coping strategies. There are many types of phobias with some very interesting names. You may have heard of arachnophobia – a fear of spiders. But have you heard of alektorophobia – a fear of chickens? Or how about albuminurophobia – a fear of kidney disease?

What follows is Jane's description of her claustrophobia – a fear of confined spaces:

"Whenever I think about getting in a lift or being in a crowded store, I just go to pieces. The other day, I was on my way to a meeting with some work colleagues. We parked the car in a large multi-storey car park on the top floor. I just couldn't get in the car park lift and told my colleagues I would walk down. They must have thought I was strange and quite frankly I'm beginning to think I am too. I have started to avoid some work situations. I just can't go on like this."

3. Social phobia

A social phobia is an irrational fear of social situations. This kind of phobia is different from a specific phobia because the situations the sufferer fears can be wide ranging. A social phobia is more intense than just shyness. Typically, sufferers assume they will be judged and evaluated negatively. They view public situations such as attending parties or giving speeches as extremely painful and distressing, and live with a constant fear of being judged, observed, remarked upon and rejected. People with social phobia can also experience an irrational fear of doing something stupid or embarrassing. Social phobia can cause a person to avoid social gatherings altogether in order to reduce their perceived fear of looking foolish and feeling embarrassed.

Barry's fear of social events:

"I'm terrified of saying the wrong thing and looking stupid. I don't get so nervous when talking to one person, although even that can sometimes cause a problem. However, when I'm introduced to a crowd of people, I shake and blush. I just find it so difficult to mix and chat with people. If I'm at a social gathering, I cannot hold a drink without shaking. I'm always afraid I will say something stupid and look like a fool. Last year, I dropped a glass of wine at a party. I got some really bad looks from people and since then I have turned down quite a few invitations. My fear of looking like a fool just seems to be getting worse."

4. Agoraphobia

Agoraphobia is a panic disorder that is characterised by anxiety in situations where the sufferer perceives certain environments as dangerous or uncomfortable. It is not only a fear of open spaces but also the fear of being in unfamiliar places and of leaving safe places such as one's home. Many people with agoraphobia are afraid they'll lose control. In this sense, it has characteristics that are similar to a panic attack and the two often go together. Not everyone with agoraphobia is frightened to go beyond their front door. However, many fear mixing with groups of people, be they friends or strangers.

Jenny's experience of agoraphobia:

"Every morning and night, I experience waves of panic and anxiety. I am barely able to leave the house. When on my own, I will only venture as far as the local shop and that is a huge ordeal. I'm better if accompanied by a good friend or my husband. But it's been months since I mixed with more that two or three people at a time. I buy most of my big shops online as just the thought of a trip to the supermarket fills me with dread."

5. Panic disorder

Panic attacks are intense physical and mental feelings of apprehension or impending disaster. Physical feelings can be varied and include:

- Heart palpitations
- Irregular heart rhythms
- Chest pains
- Breathlessness
- Intense feelings of fear
- Light-headedness and dizziness
- Feeling like you're outside yourself
- Sense of unreality

A panic attack can seem to come out of the blue and the

feelings and sensations can be very powerful, sudden and scary. People will often over-breath and hyperventilate during a panic attack, which increases the distress experienced. Although people feel an overwhelming sense of fear and unreality, a panic attack is not dangerous and shouldn't cause any physical harm. They can last anything between five and 20 minutes.

Teresa's experience of panic attacks:

"The first time I experienced a panic attack, I was at work. I remember it was a hot sticky summer's day and we didn't have air conditioning in our office. I got so nervous that I had to leave the office and go to see the nurse in occupational health. She helped me to calm down by showing me how to breathe into a paper bag. Since then, I have had other panic attacks and the first thing I want to do is get out of the situation that I believe is causing it, often crowded places, especially when it's hot and there's not much air. However, now that I'm having therapy and learning new coping skills, the panic is less frequent."

6. Post-traumatic stress disorder

Post-traumatic stress disorder (PTSD) is a reaction to a very traumatic event. Most people will avoid traumas such as rape, serious traffic accidents or witnessing a major disaster. However, those who are unfortunate enough to experience a major life trauma followed by PTSD will need outside help because the effects can last for years.

Symptoms of PTSD can be psychological and physical.

Re-experiencing the trauma:

For the majority of sufferers, this is probably the most common symptom of PTSD. A person will vividly re-live the event in the form of flashbacks, nightmares or involuntary images. Some people will even re-experience the physical pain associated with the trauma.

Feeling anxious and on edge all the time:

Another common symptom is to feel continually on edge, which can make it very difficult to relax. A person may also feel angry, irritable, and have difficulty concentrating and sleeping. They may become prone to angry outbursts and even violence.

Avoiding situations and people that bring back memories of the event:

People will often avoid situations and people that remind them of the traumatic event. Sometimes, people will avoid talking about the event and push traumatic memories and feelings away. This emotional numbing can lead a person to become withdrawn, isolated and depressed. They may even withdraw from everyday events such as work and social activities. People can also experience anxiety, phobias and go on to abuse drugs and alcohol to numb the pain.

Sasha's experience of PTSD:

"Three years ago, I was a passenger in a minicab that slid on ice and crashed into a tree. I was knocked out because the next thing I remember was waking up in the back of an ambulance. Tragically, the driver was killed. I broke a wrist

and suffered injuries to my neck and back. I went back to work a month later, but started to experience panic attacks. I also began having reoccurring nightmares about the crash. I was diagnosed with PTSD and saw a therapist. Although I still experience the odd low day, I am well on my way to recovery."

7. Obsessive compulsive disorder

Obsessive compulsive disorder (OCD) is a destructive anxiety in which a person experiences a compulsion to carry out certain acts or to focus on specific mental images or thoughts in order to relieve symptoms of anxiety. The behaviours and fears associated with OCD can seem confusing and bizarre to onlookers as well as to the sufferer. OCD typically has two parts: obsessions and compulsions. While similar, they present in different forms.

Compulsions – a compulsion can either be overt or covert:

Overt: Repeatedly checking the front door is locked

Covert: Repeating a specific phrase in the mind over and over again

Obsessions – these are uncontrollable thoughts, images, worries and fears that are unwanted and disturbing. The obsessive thoughts interfere with day-to-day life, making them very hard to ignore. Not produced by choice, the obsessive thinking can be very intrusive. Nevertheless, the person with OCD recognises that these often distressing and sometimes ugly thoughts are their own and not controlled by anyone or anything on the outside.

Another example of an obsession would be worrying that your partner might get very ill and die, while a compulsion would be feeling anxious if you don't switch off every electrical appliance before you leave the house. In many cases, the feelings are linked – those with OCD may feel as though they have to switch off every electrical device before going out, otherwise their partner may get very ill and die.

Gloria's experience of OCD:

"I had a fear that all sorts of bugs and rats might infect me and make me ill. I was constantly cleaning, scrubbing and disinfecting things around the house. I would only eat off paper plates and cups, and use plastic knives and forks. Whenever I went out, I experienced panic attacks. My relationship with my husband was severely tested. I didn't want him to go anywhere without me. I feared something bad would happen to him. I started cutting myself off from family and friends, and stayed at home. Medication and cognitive therapy have helped me. It took a year, but I'm now functioning so much better."

Self-help for anxiety

Uncomfortable feelings of anxiety can often be put down to a dreaded event that people expect will happen. When experiencing anxiety, people typically anticipate the worst. They will overestimate the risks and danger of an event while underestimating their ability to cope. This is sometimes referred to as catastrophising, an irrational form of thinking in which people believe that something is far worse than it actually is.

When we engage in catastrophic thinking, we make a horror out of a situation. For example, a student may fail one particular exam. She then tells herself that she is a complete and utter failure and that she will fail her final year and never go to university. No matter how much reassurance her teachers and friends give her, she insists there's no solution. In reality, it may only be a temporary situation, and there are things she can do to change this. This form of catastrophising takes a current situation and blows it way out of proportion.

Another form of catastrophising focuses more on future events. This kind of catastrophising occurs when we look to the future and tell ourselves: *"Whatever could go wrong, WILL go wrong."* Because we believe this, we create a self-fulfilling prophecy. Catastrophising can limit a person's opportunities in life. It can affect their outlook and create feelings of failure, disappointment and underachievement.

Rethink it!

Write down your catastrophic thinking and challenge it.

First, identify when you are catastrophising. Then write down your negative thoughts about events. Write down what happened as accurately as possible, your thoughts about the situation, and how you reacted/behaved.

Over time, you will be able to see a pattern and the situation and thoughts that trigger your catastrophising. You can then challenge and change the catastrophic thoughts that lead to feelings of anxiety.

For example:

"I failed my history exam. I'm useless, a total failure. I'm going to fail my final year and never make it to university."

Challenge-

"No, that's not true. Everybody makes mistakes – I'm only human. It's unfortunate that I failed that particular exam, but it's just one exam and it doesn't mean I won't go to university. If I need to, I can retake it."

Catastrophic thinking

"I can't believe I haven't made a sale for a week! My boss is going to fire me for sure this time."

Challenge-

"I haven't made a sale but neither has anyone else in the department. I have made many sales this year, but now happens to be a slow period. My boss understands this and I have no evidence he will fire me."

Make your aim to reduce your catastrophic thinking as much as you can. By challenging your irrational thoughts, you will find your catastrophising reduces in frequency and strength and before you know it, you won't be feeling as anxious.

The 'Stop' technique can reduce anxiety

Thought-stopping is a technique popularised by a behavioural therapist named Joseph Wolpe in the 1950s. It is primarily used for the treatment of obsessive thoughts and phobias. It can be adapted to ease anxiety by adding extra elements. It works as follows:

1. As soon as you feel the slightest feeling of unease, say the word *"Stop"* to yourself – if you're on your own, you may find it more effective to say it out loud. If you're in the company of others, say it silently but with passion, as if you are saying it aloud. You can say it with as much force as you like. Some people also find it useful to imagine a cannon being fired at the same time, while others think of a red traffic light. You can add phrases such as *"Stop, this is nonsense"* or *"Stop, I don't need this."* However, don't make the mistake of putting yourself down. It is the catastrophic thoughts and feelings you are silencing, not yourself.

2. Next, focus all your attention on sights and sounds in your immediate vicinity. By doing this, you give your mind something external to focus on, instead of your negative thoughts and feelings. Use as many of your senses as you can – sight, sound, smell, even taste – to bring yourself into the present moment.

3. Next, use a breathing technique to calm yourself down. Breathe in slowly and evenly through your nose, exhaling even more slowly through your mouth. As you

breathe in, silently say the word *"calm"* to yourself. As you breathe out, say the word *"relax"*. Try to make the out-breath up to twice as long as your in-breath. The idea is to empty your lungs of old air and make room in your lungs for fresh oxygen-rich air. One way to achieve this is to slow down the speed you repeat the word, *"relax"*. *"Calm"* on the in-breath, *"R-e-l-a-x"* on the out-breath. If your mind wanders, bring your attention to your words as you breathe in calm and out r-e-l-a-x-e-d.

Practise relaxation techniques

When practiced regularly, relaxation techniques such as mindfulness meditation, progressive muscle relaxation and deep breathing can reduce anxiety symptoms and increase feelings of relaxation and emotional wellbeing. You will find relaxation exercises explained later in *Relax, Breathe and Stay Sane.*

Adopt healthy eating habits

Start the day right with breakfast, and continue with lunch and an evening meal. Going too long without eating leads to low blood sugar, which can make you feel more anxious. Eating regular meals will help to stabilise your blood sugar level and your mood. Aim for three meals a day, with a healthy snack mid-morning and mid-afternoon to boost your metabolism and ensure energy is used effectively.

Exercise

Exercise is a natural anxiety reliever. To achieve the maximum benefit, aim for at least 30 minutes of aerobic exercise each day or every other day. It really can make you feel better because it releases endorphins, the body's natural anti-depressant hormone.

Do a form of exercise you find enjoyable. Swimming, walking or riding a bicycle are wonderful ways of relieving anxiety.

I have found that people with anxiety really benefit from fast-paced walking, as it gets them out of the house, requires little in the way of preparation and needs no special exercise equipment.

Make your exercise aerobic by walking briskly, but be gentle with yourself. Start gradually and build up the amount of exercise. Don't expect to be an Olympic champion. Perhaps you can join an aerobic or swimming class.

When starting any form of new exercise, it is always advisable to consult your doctor first. If you experience chest pain or any other distressing symptoms, seek medical attention.

Do not avoid your fears

Do not avoid situations in which you experience anxiety. Instead, gradually expose yourself to the feared situation. That way you will unlearn your old ways of thinking that feed the negative feelings. Anxiety will then reduce until it leaves you completely. However, this needs to be undertaken with some care and in gradual steps.

Depression

Depression affects approximately one fifth of adults in the UK. Some people still think depression is trivial and not a genuine health condition, but they are wrong. While everyone can feel low, down in the dumps or *'can't be bothered'* from time to time, clinical depression is an illness, and it is one of the most painful mood states that can be experienced.

The intense feelings of sadness associated with depression can last for weeks, months and even years, with the symptoms of depression being both emotional and physical.

When people experience low mood or are clinically depressed, they will quite often have a critical way of thinking about themselves, other people and the future.

Typical depressed thoughts can include:

About self:

- I'm useless
- I'm a failure
- I'm ugly

About others

- Family and friends think I'm a burden
- People don't like me
- Other people can cope – why can't I?

The future

- Things will never get better
- There's no point in trying

Other symptoms of depression include:

- Feelings of hopelessness
- Loss of interest in life
- Fatigue
- Difficulty concentrating
- Lack of motivation
- Lack of self-worth
- Feelings of guilt
- Suicidal thoughts and feelings
- Disturbed sleep
- A change in appetite – overeating or under-eating
- Weight change
- Loss of libido

If you're experiencing some of these symptoms, you may

be depressed. However, it's important to resist the temptation to self-diagnose. Depression requires medical and psychological evaluation. If you are feeling depressed, then please make an appointment to see your doctor.

Rethink it!

If you're experiencing depression, you're probably aware that your thinking is overly negative and unrealistic. Indeed depression seems to cloud everything, including the way you see yourself, the situations you encounter, and your expectations for the future.

Regardless of the type of depression, your thoughts play an important role in maintaining and even deepening your depression.

Trying to think *'happy thoughts'* won't really help. Instead, use the techniques described in Part One, *What do you say when you talk to yourself?* This can go a long way towards helping you replace negative thoughts with more balanced thoughts.

In addition the following ideas can help:

Stop being so hard on yourself

Ask yourself if you'd say what you're thinking about yourself to someone else. If not, why the double standard? Just because you think you're weak, stupid, a failure or emotionally flawed doesn't make those thoughts true.

Challenge and change the harsh and cruel statements to ones that offer kinder and, crucially, more realistic descriptions and explanations. Write down thoughts of feeling helpless or hopeless.

Be especially aware of making sweeping generalisations after one specific bad event, so that even your whole future appears to be terrible.

From: *"I lost my job – I'll never have a good job again."*

To: *"Just because I lost my job, it doesn't follow that I won't find another. I've found jobs before and I will do so again."*

From: *"I'm useless – a total failure and I will never recover!"*

To: *"I may be feeling useless, but that doesn't make me useless. I feel like a failure because I am currently depressed. I've got over bouts of depression before and will do so again."*

Take care of yourself

Exercise – if you're depressed the last thing you may feel like doing is exercise. However, as with anxiety, exercise really can help you to feel better because it releases endorphins, the body's natural anti-depressant hormone.

Take things one day at a time and reward yourself for each accomplishment. The steps may seem small, but they'll quickly add up.

Avoid alcohol and illegal drugs

It's important to avoid alcohol as well as illegal and some non-prescription drugs. Alcohol and illegal drugs affect the body's central nervous system and can cause depression. What's more, they inhibit the effectiveness of anti-depressant medication as well as some other medicines.

There is also some evidence to suggest that products containing aspartame, such as sweeteners, can make symptoms of depression worse. If in doubt, speak to your doctor.

Talk to supportive relatives and friends

Getting support from trusted relatives and friends can play a big part in helping you to cope with and overcome depression. When isolated, it can be difficult to keep perspective and sustain the effort required to beat depression. Paradoxically, the nature of depression can make it difficult to ask for help. However, isolation and loneliness make low mood and depression even worse, so keeping close relationships is important.

The thought of reaching out to even close family members may seem difficult. You may feel like you are being a burden or somehow not worth the effort. Remember, you are probably thinking about yourself in this way due to your depression. Let the people you love and trust know what you're going though. Don't feel that you cannot ask for the help and support you need. You may have retreated from your closest relationships, but these people can help support you while you get through this difficult and challenging time.

Although it may feel like the last thing you want to do, try to keep up with social activities such as hobbies. Challenge yourself to do things, even though you may think you're not in the mood. Don't wait until you feel like it. Being around other people will help you to feel less depressed, and you'll be surprised at how much better you feel once you start to actually do things and engage with others. You'll begin to feel more upbeat and energetic as you make time for enjoyable activities.

Create a structure to your day. By drawing up a plan detailing what to do and when to do it, you'll find it easier to become more active, which will increase your energy levels and decrease depressive thinking. Doing even the most straightforward activities – as long as they're practical, realistic and pleasurable – improves motivation and leads to a greater sense of achievement.

Eat a healthy diet and watch your eating habits

Depression can affect your eating habits. You may find you lose your appetite or you lack the motivation to prepare food. Some people find their appetite for unhealthy foods increases and they end up gaining weight. Both of these habits tend to exacerbate depression. Blood sugar levels can go up and down and can affect your mood, making you feel even more miserable. Eating regular meals will help to stabilise your blood sugar level and your mood. Aim for three meals a day – breakfast, lunch and an evening meal, with a healthy snack mid-morning and mid-afternoon to boost your metabolism and ensure energy is used effectively. If you find it hard to eat, try eating little and often.

Regular sleep time

A good night's sleep is especially important for those suffering from depression. However, too much sleep can make matters worse. A regular sleeping pattern is important in managing depression, which means going to bed and getting up at approximately the same times each day. Before turning in, allow yourself some time to wind down. A warm relaxing bath can help. You could include some essential oils, although do seek the advice of a doctor or qualified therapist, as they should not be used if you are pregnant, take certain medicines, or have certain medical conditions. A warm milky drink and a light snack just before bed can also help. If you find you don't fall asleep within 20-30 minutes, don't lie in bed tossing and turning. Instead, get up, go into another room and read until you feel sleepy.

Above all seek help

It is essential to look after yourself - even in good times, but it is especially important when experiencing emotional difficulties such as depression.

If you're finding it hard, ask your partner or a close friend or relative to help you eat well and avoid alcohol, caffeine and illegal drugs. Challenge your negative thinking, embrace the sunlight and take regular exercise. To feel well, you need to eat well, exercise well and sleep well.

Make no mistake – clinical depression is an illness and it is one of the most painful mood states that can be experienced. It requires medical and psychological evaluation. The symptoms can be both emotional and physical and seriously affect a person's ability to function. It is the illness itself that can lead you to think of depression as a sign of weakness and to label yourself as useless or a lost cause. If you find your depression is getting worse, seek professional help. Needing additional support doesn't mean you're weak. With the right help, you can overcome depression, enabling you to not only feel better but, most importantly, get better.

Anger

Anger is a basic human emotion, a physical and psychological response to threats and attacks, injustice and disappointment. Anger can express itself in a multitude of forms, ranging from irritation to damming rage. It can also be quite subtle, manifesting in resentment that festers just below the surface over many years. Feeling angry is neither good nor bad. It is how you choose to handle it that makes the difference. If anger isn't dealt with in a healthy way, if it is too extreme, occurs at inappropriate times or lasts too long, it can have a self-defeating and destructive effect on daily life, relationships, achievements and mental wellbeing.

Myths about anger

Holding onto anger is bad for your health – we must let anger out.

Some people would have us believe that experiencing anger and holding onto it is bad for our health. However, this is not strictly true. After all, there are times when it is inappropriate to express our feelings and we may have to refrain from revealing that we're angry. The issue for our health is chronic anger, which can contribute to heart disease, high blood pressure, raised cholesterol, headaches, and stomach and digestive problems.

Human beings are aggressive by default.

While it is a given that humans have the capacity to try to settle differences through conflict, they also have the ability to resolve issues through peace and communication. Aggression is a learned behaviour, acted out by individuals who have poor control over their emotions and have used and got away with it in the past.

To get rid of anger, rage and hostility, it should always be expressed.

Research into anger has shown that this is largely not the case. Constantly venting anger every time a person gets upset can actually increase hostility and frustration.

It is not always beneficial to say what you feel. While it is useful and often important to express feelings in a respectful manner, people can sometimes do this in a destructive way, falsely believing they are being assertive, when, in reality, they are being thoughtless and aggressive. It is important to think through what you want to say before speaking, rather than diving in and hurting someone's feelings just to relieve your anger.

Why manage your anger?

As aforementioned, it is how we choose to manage our anger that makes a difference. Chronic anger that is not resolved can lead to extreme stress, heart disease and strokes. We all experience anger, but it is when it becomes pent up that problems can occur. Learning to control anger and channelling it into positive coping skills can help to resolve issues and ultimately lead to a healthier and happier life.

Rethink it!

1. Think about the situations that trigger your anger and rate them

Spend some time thinking about the situations that make you angry, such as work, your partner, children or parents. Then identify the degree of anger you feel on a scale from one to five (one being mild anger or annoyance and five being damming anger or rage). By rating your responses in this way, you'll learn which situations trigger your anger and how often.

The higher the score, the more likely you are to have 'anger demands' and the more you will need to challenge and change these demands. You can do so by using the exercises in Part One, Section 3, *How demands lead to misery,* to reduce your anger. Over time, your rating of a particular situation will change.

When your score goes down, make a note of how you changed it. If your level of anger rises, look again at your demands and the hostile thoughts you may be holding onto. Once you have been monitoring the situations and triggers for a week or so, you may see that you are angry more often that you thought, or you may be able to pinpoint a pattern.

This gives you the chance to deal with your anger in a more effective way and to resolve some of the issues that are keeping you cross.

2. Buy yourself some time

If you feel a well of anger bubbling away, pause, take a deep breath in and an even longer one out. Once you feel your body starting to relax, think about the consequences of blowing up with damning anger and instead choose a more appropriate way to respond. Here's how:

- Count to 10 then act.
- Take in another couple of deep breaths and, as you exhale, say the word relax to yourself.
- Scan your body for tension and let it go. If you're feeling violent and fear you might throw something or hit someone, remove yourself from the situation until you have calmed down.
- Imagine what a good friend would say to calm you down and repeat it to yourself.
- Distract yourself by going for a walk or using relaxation techniques.
- Talk to someone you trust, such as a friend or family member, to get an outside perspective on the issue.

3. Be assertive

Being assertive is a healthy way to express anger because it allows you to communicate why you're angry. Some simple but effective communication skills will enable you to be assertive and get your point across while minimising the possibility of anger and conflict:

- Speak clearly without rushing.
- Make requests rather than demands.
- Say *"I could"* and *"I might"* instead of *"I must"* or *"I should"*.

People can react negatively to criticism so it can be helpful to cushion the blow by starting with a positive statement, as the following example illustrates:

"I realise that you needed to express your point of view, but I feel upset by your remark."

This example also illustrates the use of 'I' statements instead of 'you' statements. 'You' statements are far more likely to cause the other person to become defensive. 'I' statements are a way of communicating an issue without accusing the other person of being the problem.

You can learn more about assertiveness in Part Three, Section 14: *How to be assertive*.

4. Picture yourself coping while using calming self-talk

You can use visualisation and self-talk to reduce feelings of anger. Imagery can help you to rehearse your response to situations in which you get angry, while self-talk phrases can help you to feel calm, enabling you to handle the situation effectively.

Self-help phrases should be short, instructional and

encouraging, as opposed to put-downs.

Popular self-talk

"Relax. Take a deep breath. Hold it. And let it all out."

"I really don't have to feel angry about this if I choose not to."

"I won't let him push my emotional buttons."

Be specific and stick to the point.

Keep your voice down.

Visualisation

Find a comfortable place to sit, uncross your arms and legs, and then close your eyes. Take three deep breaths and visualise a frequently occurring anger-provoking scene. Imagine yourself in that situation, seeing things through your own eyes. See and hear yourself and the other person. When you start to feel angry, repeat your calming phrases to yourself. Then imagine yourself handling things in a calm and confident way. Practise this imagery until you become calm, regardless of what you see the other person doing. If you find it difficult to use your coping statement effectively, you can say something more forceful, such as the word 'Stop', before your calming phases.

Repeat the visualisation for about five to ten minutes, two to three times a day, until you are satisfied with your improvement. Start with anger-provoking situations in which you feel relatively mild anger or annoyance and, as you become proficient at handling them, move up a level to situations that provoke stronger feelings of anger.

5. Practise listening

It is important to learn to listen to other people's opinions without jumping to conclusions. We can avoid creating anger by resisting the urge to interrupt people with our own comments and turning conversations into pressurised cross-examinations.

6. Don't take yourself too seriously

Learn to laugh at yourself. We all overreact to things that are really quite trivial. If you are always upset, you are more likely to feel and express anger. Working under time constraints, a lack of humour and too many items on your 'to do' list will keep you feeling nervous and jumpy. Learning not to take ourselves too seriously and even laughing at our overreactions to events, can often help to get rid of the anger and keep situations in perspective.

Jealousy

Do you find yourself checking your partner's phone and emails every day? Do you go through their pockets looking for evidence of wrongdoing or perhaps telephone them five times a day to find out what time they will be home? Do you feel your stomach churning whenever your partner starts talking to a member of the opposite sex? If the answer is yes to any of the above questions then jealousy may well be an issue that needs addressing.

We can all experience a small amount of jealousy within our partnerships and this may not be a bad thing as it can add some spice to our relationships, helping couples to appreciate each other and what they have. However, chronic jealousy can cause major stress-related health problems and upset for both partners and can ultimately lead to a relationship breakup. At its most extreme, people have killed because they are jealous.

What is jealousy?

Drs Robert L Leahy and Dennis D Tirch have carried out research into jealousy and describe it as *"angry agitated worry."* A universal emotion, it can also be an adaptive feeling triggered by certain factors in different cultures. There is a big difference between feeling jealous and acting on your jealousy. A relationship is more likely to get into trouble if certain behaviours are present, such as making accusations or going through a partner's trousers or handbag looking for clues. Constantly seeking reassurance from a partner is unlikely to solve the issue.

Rethink it!

For most people, distorted thinking is a major factor in maintaining their jealousy. Negative perceptions of self and of other people fuel jealousy, making a person feel bad. Changing that negative thinking into more rational thoughts is a major way of taking control of the emotion. If you examine the beliefs behind your jealous feelings, you can often eliminate some, if not all, of the jealousy.

Steps to overcome jealousy

1. Be mindful of your thoughts and feelings

If you experience feelings of jealousy, don't act on them or run away from them. Instead relax and focus on the rhythm of your breathing, the rise and the fall of your diaphragm and chest. Focus on your thoughts and feelings in a calm detached way. Your jealous thoughts are just thoughts – they are not reality. For instance, if you think your partner is interested in someone else, does it follow that she or he really is? The things we think and feel can be quite different from reality.

2. Don't remain a slave to jealous thoughts and feelings

You may find that observing your thoughts and feelings about jealousy initially causes the feelings to increase. It is important to accept that you have the emotion and to allow yourself to feel it in order to 'let it be'. Sometimes, simply taking a step back to observe that the emotion exists, rather than fighting it or pushing it away, can lead to that feeling weakening on its own, like ice melting in the sun.

3. Tackle your feelings when they arise

Question your jealousy whenever it raises its ugly head. For example, ask yourself: *"Am I feeling jealous because I feel angry or afraid? What is the reason I feel fear or anger at this time?"* By questioning the triggers behind your jealousy at the time it occurs you can begin to take positive steps to manage the feelings positively, without allowing the negative emotion that typically accompanies jealousy to get in the way.

You can ask yourself:

"Why am I feeling threatened?"

"What is it about this situation that causes me to feel jealous?"

"What specific issue is making me jealous?"

4. Don't demand certainty

Jealousy can arise when we demand certainty. For instance, we insist that we must have a guarantee that he isn't interested in another woman. Or *"I absolutely have to know that this relationship will last forever."* These demands will only increase anxiety and suspicion. We need to accept that uncertainty is part of life and that, even though we may desire certainty, it can never be guaranteed. Indeed, demanding a guarantee may lead to a negative self-fulfilling prophecy.

5. Don't make assumptions

We all have a tendency to make assumptions about things. Just because you feel there is a threat, it doesn't mean that it's genuine. Try to view the situation objectively.

Jealousy can lead to unrealistic thoughts about our relationships and a powerful imagination can result in all kinds of unproven ideas and stories. We start imagining what our partner is up to and what they're thinking and saying about us. We may believe that our partner should never be attracted to anyone else and that our feeling of jealousy is evidence that she or he is up to no good. You may run yourself down, believing nobody could love you as you have so little to offer. However, there are many effective ways of dealing with feelings of insecurity within relationships:

- Praise each other on a regular basis and refrain from criticism and labelling.
- Plan and share positive experiences together on a regular basis, such as days out.
- Learn how to share responsibility in solving problems and tackle issues together.

By refusing to make assumptions about your partner, you will lift a great weight from your shoulders and see life as it is, rather than how your jealousy wants you to see it.

6. Learn to trust yourself

If you learn to trust yourself then you can begin to trust others.

Begin by writing a list of all your good points and put the list up somewhere you can see it. You need to remind yourself that you have talent, skills and positive features. Don't compare yourself to others, but instead tell yourself daily that you have what it takes to lead a positive and fulfilling life. Practise rational healthy thinking every day and, in time, the healthier thoughts will replace the jealous feelings, helping you to become a more resilient and capable person who is not prone to jealousy.

Relax, breathe and stay sane

Many people hold the attitude that relaxation is unnecessary while others may think that they do not have the time to relax. Some people believe that relaxation is only for winding down at the end of a hard day, perhaps with an alcoholic drink or watching their favourite soap opera. One of my clients believed that time spent following a relaxation procedure would impede his efficiency at work, but after a few weeks practice he felt more alert and better able to concentrate. Relaxation can also:

- Reduce your anxiety
- Eliminate fatigue
- Improve physical and mental performance
- Help you get to sleep
- Manage pain
- Lower blood pressure
- Manage irritable bowel syndrome

Relax and Rethink it!

If you are willing to give yourself 4 to 5 minutes a few times a day practicing a simple but highly effective relaxation method you will be surprised to discover the health giving benefits you can achieve.

Even the following 2 minute mini-relaxation technique

practiced 4 to 5 times a day can help you feel more alert, better able to focus and, above all, less stressed.

This is how it is done:

1 Sit in a comfortable chair or lay back on your bed

2 Relax and close your eyes

3 Breathe slowly.

4 Let all the muscles of your body r-e-l-a-x

5 Imagine a pleasant scene

If you practice that technique for 2 to 5 minutes, 4 or 5 times a day you will soon discover that you are feeling less irritable and stressed and that the positive feelings created from the pleasant scene stay with you.

Picture your stress away

You can use your mind to help you relax by creating pleasant images in your imagination.

This is called visualization and can involve all of your senses. For example, if you were to imagine yourself on a beach you could picture the sand, feel the warmth of the sun, hear the sound of the sea and smell the salt air.

Imagery can also be used to create and recreate emotions. For instance, you could imagine a past experience when you felt very calm and relaxed.

Lisa's imaginary bolt-hole

Lisa uses the power of visualization to create her own imaginary safe place. Whenever Lisa feels that stress is getting the better of her she goes to this place in her mind to recharge her emotional battery.

This is how it is done:

1 Sit in a comfortable place and close your eyes.

2 Focus on the rhythm of your breathing.

3 In your mind create a picture of a comfortable relaxing place.

4 Allow yourself to feel relaxed and safe in this place. Think of it as somewhere where you can be yourself and let go of all your worries.

5 When you're ready, open your eyes.

You can go to your bolt-hole whenever you feel the need. You can use it as a place to resolve problems, to think things through or just switch off. The more you practice, the easier it will become.

Scan your stress away

A fast and effective way to check for stress is to use a technique called scanning. The idea is to mentally scan through your body from the top of your head to the tips of your toes to discover where you are holding onto tension. Whether you are driving to work or waiting at a supermarket checkout, scanning is easy to practice. The basic idea is to direct your attention throughout your body, find your tension and then let it go.

You do it like this:

1 Spend a few moments focusing on the rhythm of your breathing.

2 Breath in and mentally scan an area of your body for tension.

3 Breathe out, relaxing the tense area.

4 Move on to the next area of your body repeating the process.

Scan your body at regular intervals throughout the day. You can remind yourself to do so with an alarm-message on your phone or putting a note in your office or home.

Picture yourself coping

Negativity can feed on itself. So if you are always thinking the worst then you may actually talk yourself into more than your fair share of bad experiences. You can use visualization to cope with a situation that you fear.

This is how you do it:

1 Sit in a comfortable position and close your eyes.

2 Vividly imagine the situation you are anxious about.

3 Feel your anxiety rise.

4 Now picture yourself coping with the situation.

5 Imagine that you are talking to yourself in a reassuring way while breathing calmly.

6 Use coping statements such as:

"This is just anxiety it will soon pass."

"I know I will be ok."

"This is not as bad as I think it is."

7 When you feel your anxiety decrease open your eyes.

Practice the exercise unhurriedly every day for approximately 5 minutes. If you have a stressful situation coming up, allow as much preparation time as possible. You should start to notice a change in your anxiety after about 30 days.

Breathing is one of life's most important activities yet something few of us really think about. Most of us do not breathe deeply enough; our fast-paced stressful life has created a nation of stressed out anxious, shallow breathers. Our breathing pattern is often disrupted by changes in emotion. For instance if you are anxious, you may tend to hold your breath and speak in a high–pitched voice as you exhale. If you are depressed, you may tend to sigh and speak in a low–pitched voice as you exhale.

Changing your breathing so that you use your diaphragm can lower stress, anxiety and even high blood pressure.

If practiced over time this deep diaphragmatic breathing can result in improved energy throughout the day.

It can also:

- Reduce stress and anger
- Improve relaxation
- Help overcome fears
- Even assist those with Post Traumatic Stress Disorder

The key to deep breathing is to learn how to breathe deeply from the abdomen. Here are two techniques that can teach you to do just that.

Technique 1

A. While standing, place both hands on your lower stomach.

B. Begin to inhale while imagining that your stomach is being blown up like a balloon*. As you inhale your hands should move outwards as you breathe in slowly to a silent count of 4.

As you exhale you should draw your stomach in and your hands should move inwards while you exhale to a silent count of 5 to 6.

*This will allow the diaphragm to expand and enable air to flow all the way to the bottom of the lungs

Technique 2

A. Lie on your back on a flat but comfortable surface.

B. Place your right hand on your stomach and your left hand on your chest.

C. As you inhale your right hand should rise while your left hand remains relatively motionless as you breathe in to a silent count of 4.

D. As you exhale, your right hand should fall as you breathe out to a silent count of 5 to 6.

Try to practice at least once or twice a day at a time when you can relax, relatively free from distraction. This will help to develop a more relaxed breathing habit. The key to progress is to practice, so try to set aside some time each day.

Once you have learned and practiced these deep-breathing techniques you can do them while standing, sitting or lying down.

Practice mindfulness

Mindfulness is a type of meditation that involves focusing your mind on the present moment. You become aware of your actions in the here and now. You don't judge – you just observe. To be mindful is to be aware of your thoughts and actions in this present moment, without judging yourself. Although a simple concept it is quite challenging. It is natural for our minds to judge our experiences as good, bad or neutral. There is now a growing amount of research suggesting that mindfulness meditation may improve mood, decrease stress, and boost immune function.

What follows is a simple mindfulness practice:

1 Start by paying attention to an everyday experience without drifting into thoughts of the past or worries about the future. The idea is to not be caught up with thoughts or opinions about what's going on.

2 Stand still or sit down and simply pay attention to your breathing. Focus on the sensation of the air moving in and out of your body, as well as the rising and falling of your diaphragm and chest. Notice the air entering your nostrils

and leaving your mouth. Don't judge, just observe.

3 Observe your thoughts – simply watch them come and go. These may be thoughts of worry, anxiety, despair or optimism – don't ignore them or fight them, just observe them without judgment.

4 If you find yourself getting carried away in your thoughts, observe where your mind went off to, without judging, and simply return to your breathing. Remember not to be hard on yourself if this happens.

5 As the time comes to a close, sit for a minute or two, becoming aware of where you are. Get up gradually.

On other occasions, you should become mindful of everyday tasks such as making the bed – notice the feel of the quilt, the smell of fresh sheets or the movement of your hand as you make the bed. When you focus your awareness on the here and now, you reduce worries, relieve stress and improve your mood.

You may find it beneficial to take a course in mindfulness meditation. By being *"present in the moment"* you can reduce the symptoms of depression, stress and even physical pain.

Part 3

Changing Your Behaviour

How to stop smoking
Psychological strategies that work

Many people don't try to stop smoking because they think it's too hard, while others have made attempts and failed. Some people have managed to stop, only to start smoking again two, three or six months later. It's true that, for many smokers, quitting isn't easy. After all, the nicotine in cigarettes is an addictive drug. But don't be discouraged; millions of people have permanently quit smoking, have overcome their cravings and now live a happy smoke-free life.

I have been helping people to give up smoking successfully for thirty years. What follows are some of the tools and techniques that have helped many of my clients to kick the habit.

Rethink it!

Preparing to stop smoking

Deciding that you want to stop smoking may seem an obvious starting point. However, many people will attempt to quit because others have persistently told them they must. While stopping smoking for the sake of family and friends is a good thing, it's often not enough and can lead to feelings of deprivation and resentment. Developing strong personal reasons to stop smoking, in addition to your obligations to others, is a far stronger motivating factor in helping you to quit.

Your personal reasons could fall under various categories. For example, perhaps you want to stop as part of an overall healthy lifestyle change. Or maybe you wish to get fit. Then again, you may be thinking about the cost of smoking and want to save money. Write down a list of the positive reasons for quitting and keep that list where you can see it. Read it on a regular basis, especially when you may feel tempted to smoke.

Decide the date you're going to stop smoking and stick to it.

Mark the date in your calendar and, if you wish, tell family and friends that you're going to stop smoking on that day. Think of the day as a dividing line between the old smoking you and the new non-smoker you have decided to become. In the run up to this date, whenever you have a cigarette, tell yourself:

"This cigarette is giving me absolutely no satisfaction."

"Smoking this cigarette is an unpleasant and uncomfortable experience."

"This cigarette is making me feel ill."

Visualise yourself free from smoking.

Knowing what steps you are going to take in order to reach your goal is important for lasting change. Taking the time to picture the process will give you the opportunity to see how you will accomplish each step along the way. A creative and effective variation on this technique is to picture the end result and then look backwards at the steps you took to achieve your goal.

This is how it's done:

1 Close your eyes and imagine that you have already become a non-smoker. You are a healthier person with more energy. Your breathing is easier and you feel fresher. Notice how good it feels to have achieved your goal.

2 Now look back at what you did. Picture the step you took just before you achieved your goal, then the step before that, all the way back to the first step. Open your eyes and hold onto the feelings of achievement.

Deal with cravings

When people stop smoking, they will often experience cravings and withdrawal symptoms. This happens because the body misses its regular hits of nicotine. People often believe that feelings of withdrawal are so awful that they cannot survive without smoking. It is realistic to say that cravings are uncomfortable, but can they truly be described as awful? And if you experience a craving, is it realistic to tell yourself that in order to survive you MUST smoke?

Learn to tolerate frustration:

The psychologist Dr Albert Ellis developed a concept he

called *low frustration tolerance* (LFT). This arises when a person experiences a frustrating situation or feeling and blows it way out of proportion.

He or she will have thoughts such as:

"I can't bear it."

"I can't stand it."

"This is awful."

"This is terrible."

If you have previously failed to stop smoking, then LFT may be at the root of your broken goal. You may believe that it's just too difficult to stop smoking and that you cannot stand the unpleasant feelings associated with the cravings. Perhaps you experienced a *"day from hell"* and believe you can't stand feeling upset. You tell yourself, *"This should not be happening to me,"* and get angry and depressed. Instead of dealing with your feelings, you medicate the emotions by smoking. It is important to understand that when working towards achieving a long-term goal, there will almost inevitably be some hassles, such as emotional discomfort, along the way. When experiencing withdrawal from smoking you may tell yourself:

"I must absolutely not experience discomfort."

"These feelings of withdrawal are awful and I cannot stand them."

If you want to successfully stop smoking, you need to challenge the notion that you should not have to feel discomfort. No-one likes to feel discomfort, but can it truly be said that you can't stand it? After all, if you truly couldn't stand something, you would die. In reality, you can stand many things. What's the worst that could happen if you went without a cigarette and experienced withdrawal? Cravings are not earth shattering and the reality is that, if you step back and accept the feelings of withdrawal, they will pass within a few minutes. Try not to give in and light up a cigarette because you'll just have to deal with the withdrawal for longer.

Counteract negative self-talk with coping statements.

If you have tried to stop smoking in the past, you may have found yourself prone to temptation, especially when confronted with challenging situations. Common negative thoughts include:

"It doesn't really matter if I have just one cigarette."

"I will never stop smoking – it's hopeless and so am I."

"If I stop smoking, I will just eat more."

"I will just have a few cigarettes tonight and stop in the morning."

Should you find yourself in a difficult situation with thoughts such as these, replace them with positive coping statements such as:

"I am taking control of this habit once and for all – this means so much to me and I will succeed."

"I can stop smoking with ease. I just need to put my mind to it. I am stronger than this habit."

"Stopping smoking is my number one health priority. I can counteract any weight gain through healthy eating and exercise."

"I have made the decision to stop smoking – now is the time to change things."

When repeating these coping statements to yourself, it is essential to say them with conviction. You need to mean what you say to yourself. Write the quotes down on an index card and carry it around with you at all times. Then if you hear yourself repeating negative self-talk, you can counteract it with the appropriate coping statements.

Mentally rehearse challenging situations

You can also rehearse coping with situations that may have driven you back to smoking in the past.

This is how it's done:

1. Sit in a comfortable chair.

2 Close your eyes and imagine yourself in the difficult situation – for example, with other people who are smoking.

3 Hear yourself repeat the negative self-statement such as *"It doesn't really matter if I have just one cigarette."*

4. Forcefully and with conviction challenge the negative thought with a coping thought such as, *"I have made the decision to stop smoking – now is the time to change things."*

5 Picture a much more calm, relaxed and confident version of yourself.

6 When ready, open your eyes.

Brief relaxation

Techniques such as self-hypnosis, mindfulness, meditation and yoga can be extremely useful in reducing the stress and tension that can sometimes be experienced when stopping smoking. You can also benefit from learning a brief method of relaxation. This is especially helpful if you find yourself in a stressful situation that in the past may have triggered you to smoke. You can also practise the technique for a couple of minutes every two or three hours to keep stress at bay. All you need to do is:

1 Sit in a comfortable chair.

2 Relax and close your eyes.

3 Focus on the rhythm of your breathing.

4 Let your whole body become loose and limp.

5 Imagine a relaxing scene.

6 When ready, open your eyes.

Lapses happen

When setting goals, adopt the attitude that you're going to do the very best you can. Like many people, you may quit successfully for weeks or even months and then suddenly have a craving that you perceive to be so strong you give in. Or maybe you experience one of your trigger situations and give in to temptation.

If you slip up, it doesn't mean you're a failure. It just means you're human and slipped up this time. Take notice of when and why it happened and resolve to minimise the chances of it happening again. Doing something without demanding that you absolutely 'must' succeed all of the time takes some of the pressure off and, paradoxically, can lead to a greater chance of success.

Weight loss:
The psychological strategies that work

Have you had difficulty shedding those excess pounds? Perhaps you have lost weight in the past, only to put it all back on. Maybe you start a diet with the best of intentions, but always seem to sabotage it after a few weeks or months and then label yourself as weak, unmotivated or even stupid. If this sounds like you, then you are not alone. While losing weight is a physical issue, for many, the real difficulty lies not on the hips but in the mind. A lot of people have a deep emotional attachment to foods that they love, which cannot be easily overcome by limiting the intake of these foods. The good news is that losing weight is much easier if you are psychologically prepared for it.

It's not just about what you eat

When most people try to lose weight, they only tend to think about what they eat. Questions revolve around how much fat, protein and carbs to consume. Some may even try unhealthy fad diets. While nutritional information is very important, it's not the whole answer. What many tend to ignore is how they approach and manage the process of change. In other words, many people just don't know how to diet. It is crucial to consider changes in behaviour and strategies that encourage a new relationship with the food we eat. An increase in physical activity is also very important.

Rethink it!

What follows are self-help strategies that can assist you with losing weight and changing behaviour:

Setting goals

If you want to meet your weight loss goals, then consider setting specific goals. If your goals are specific then you are far more likely to achieve a desired outcome – for example, one of your goals may be to eat three healthy meals a day and limit eating between meals to fruit.

Write your goals down on an index card and remember to carry the card around with you. Then, if you get tempted to sway, you can remind yourself of them.

Ensure the goals are achievable

Your goals don't have to be big ones. You may find it helpful to break your goals down into small steps – for example, instead of saying, *"I am going to go to the gym every day,"* break it down into *"I will go to the gym once a week for two weeks then gradually increase my exercise and visits to the gym."*

It is important to identify when and where you are

engaging in behaviours that lead to weight gain and turn them around with little steps that you can easily handle without feeling deprived. Encouragement from another person can increase your chances of success. A therapist, coach or diet buddy can offer motivation by reminding you that your efforts are worthwhile.

Change your attitude towards food intake

If you want to lose weight, it is essential that you learn how to tell the difference between genuine hunger and an urge or craving to eat when you're not actually hungry. This can be achieved through something I call hunger awareness. By paying attention to how your stomach feels before and after a meal, you can learn what real hunger feels like. So how do you tell the difference between a genuine feeling of hunger and a strong desire or craving to eat even though your last meal may not even have been properly digested?

Most of us have memories of times we felt really hungry and times when we just wanted to eat for the sake of eating.

The following exercise will help you to distinguish between the feelings:

Close your eyes and remember a time when you genuinely hadn't eaten for many hours and felt very hungry. Can you remember that empty feeling in your stomach and how it rumbled? That is a genuine feeling of hunger and signals that you need to eat.

Now shift your attention to a time when you had just finished a large tasty meal. You know you have eaten a lot, but there is more food readily available and you want to eat it. That is not genuine hunger – it's a desire to eat more.

Let that memory fade and focus your attention on a time you felt stressed, and even though you had recently eaten, you felt a strong desire to eat cake, chocolate or some other food. Again, that is not real hunger – it's a craving.

Now you have a better idea of the difference between genuine hunger, desire and cravings, you can become more aware of when you're genuinely hungry and when you're eating for emotional or other unhelpful reasons. I'm not saying you have to be ravenous before you can eat your planned meal – however, by being aware of the differences you will know when you are likely to sabotage your diet.

It is also important not to eat while standing next to the refrigerator, driving, working at your desk or watching television. Instead, sit down at a table that is meant for eating. Take in a slow, deep breath, and breathe out, relaxing as you do so. Then eat slowly, remembering to chew your food well. That way, you will feel full on a smaller amount of food.

More about cravings

Have you ever heard yourself saying?

"I must eat now."

"It's terrible to wait till dinnertime."

"I must have my daily fix of chocolate right NOW."

When you embark on a weight loss programme, it is natural to experience some discomfort and food cravings.

The good news is you can challenge the notion that you *"should not have to experience food cravings."* Food cravings can be uncomfortable, but they are tolerable, especially when compared with significant pain such as a broken arm or leg.

What you say to yourself can influence your behaviour and emotions in significant ways. Some thoughts will block you from achieving your weight loss goals, while others will empower you to achieve them.

If you do experience food cravings, you can tell yourself that:

"This craving is tolerable and will soon pass. By not giving in to this craving, I feel a great sense of achievement. I may feel some mild discomfort, but will feel far worse if I give in to temptation."

Food cravings always pass, provided you make a firm decision not to give in. Instead, distract yourself with other activities. To take your mind away from the craving, focus on something that you enjoy doing. Going for a short, gentle stroll in the fresh air can clear your mind. This helps if you're feeling stressed, anxious or low. Walking is calming, and getting active outdoors will lift your mood much more than giving in to a food craving – as will reading an enjoyable book, taking a bath or, if it's a late-night craving, simply going to bed. Getting enough sleep each night is a vitally important replenishing exercise that gives us the right mind set to handle cravings.

You can also remain passive and watch your cravings rise, peak and then subside, without judging or doing anything about them. Once you realise that you can take control of your cravings, rather than being at their beck and call, you will feel liberated. Once a craving subsides, congratulate yourself on a job well done.

Picture yourself sticking to your weight loss goals

For some, eating out can be a challenge. You may be invited to a dinner party where well-meaning friends are likely to tempt you with mouth-watering foods. Before you go to the party, use some mental imagery to rehearse sticking to your weight loss goal.

This is how it's done:

1 Sit in a comfortable chair and close your eyes.

2 Take a deep breath in and, as you breathe out, relax and release any tension in your body.

3 Picture a calm and confident version of yourself sticking to your weight loss goal. For example, imagine a delicious, hot, creamy dessert. You can smell it and almost taste it. Now see yourself firmly but politely refusing a repeated offer of the cream dessert. Get in touch with a genuine feeling of conviction. You mean it this time. Feel good that you have refused to give in to temptation.

4 Open your eyes

By using mental imagery often, and especially before a challenging situation, success is far more likely.

Exercise creates positive feelings

Do you stop yourself from taking regular exercise? Perhaps you think that in order to start exercising you have to feel in the mood. But that's like putting the cart before the horse. Instead, tell yourself that the hardest part is getting started. Get in touch with the positive good feelings that come once you have exercised and focus on that feeling. Remind yourself that your reluctance will evaporate once you get started.

Keeping a record of your progress can help

Keeping a journal detailing what you eat, how much you exercise, your emotions, and your weight and measurements can help. Studies show that keeping track of this information helps promote positive behaviours and minimises the unhealthy ones. There are even computer, tablet and phone apps designed for this very purpose. Simply knowing that you're tracking your food intake could help you resist that tempting unhealthy snack.

How to be assertive

Being assertive doesn't come naturally to everyone. Many people communicate in a way that is too passive, while others have a style that is too aggressive. An assertive style is the happy medium between these two.

Being assertive is an important communication skill in

which you express yourself efficiently and stand up for yourself and your point of view, while also respecting the rights and beliefs of other people. A lack of assertiveness can lead to low confidence and self-worth. It is often associated with stress, depression, anxiety and anger issues. It can also lead to relationship difficulties and problems at work, as well as a multitude of other issues. Overcoming these difficulties may seem like an uphill struggle; however, with the right approach and techniques, you can learn to become a more confident, assertive person.

What stops people from being assertive?

Assertiveness is a life skill that enables people to manage their thoughts, actions and feelings, sometimes in very challenging situations. Many people struggle to be assertive for a number of reasons. Some believe that others will disapprove if they do not do the things demanded of them. They think that others will be hurt and angry if they say no to a request. They may be so afraid of rejection and being on their own that they swallow their feelings and put up with abuse, rather than run the risk of rejection. Some have an excessive need to please other people and to meet everyone else's expectations, afraid that people will disapprove if they expressed their own ideas and feelings. They may also believe that the people they care about would be hurt and couldn't take it if told an honest truth.

Some people believe that other individuals are more important than them and should come first. They may even think they do not have the right to stand up for themselves and express their own needs and opinions. Others may not even be aware of what they want out of life and so go along with people who have stronger opinions. Further barriers to assertiveness may include high levels of anxiety, fear and a lack of effective self-expression skills.

Don't confuse assertiveness with aggressive behaviour

Many people confuse assertiveness with aggression. An aggressive response contains a hostile element in which an individual attempts to satisfy personal needs without respect or taking the needs of others into account. They may speak loudly and try to be dominant, bullying others into doing what they want. They may be prone to angry outbursts that may make them feel powerful, but are inevitably destructive with potentially damaging consequences. At the other end of the spectrum, people can be too passive, speaking quietly and making themselves seem physically small and timid; they may let others overpower them and avoid making any decisions, often for fear of criticism or rejection.

By contrast, assertiveness is based on balance. It requires being forthright about your wants and needs, while still considering the rights, needs and wants of others. When you are assertive, you ask for what you want, while recognising that you don't always get it.

Rethink it!

Effective assertiveness techniques

The following skills can enable you to be assertive and get your point across while minimising the possibility of conflict. By standing tall, yet still being open and relaxed, you will be making a stand through your posture. You will also be communicating to the other person that you are confident. Don't smile too much or nod too much, and maintain direct eye contact – do not look down at the floor.

The broken record technique

The broken record technique involves repeating what you want, time and time again, without raising the tone of your voice, becoming angry, irritated, or distracted by side issues. The technique teaches you to be persistent in saying what you want, and helps you deal with people who try to manipulate you.

Example:

"I find it a little insensitive and slightly rude when you interrupt me when I'm speaking. I would be very grateful if you could please let me speak without interrupting. Thank you."

The other person may challenge you so calmly but assertively repeat your point. Remember, you remain persistent and keep saying what you want over and over without showing anger or annoyance and without raising your voice.

This example also illustrates the use of 'I' statements instead of 'you' statements. 'You' statements are far more likely to cause the other person to become defensive. 'I' statements are a way of communicating an issue without accusing the other person of being the problem.

Contrast the following:

'You' statements

"You always have to be asked to clean the flat."

"You never ask how I am."

"You never finish work on time."

'I' statements

"I would be very grateful if you could help me clean the flat."

"I would really like you to ask how I got on at my hospital appointment."

"I am getting held up with my work, as I don't have that report yet. Can you tell me when it will be ready please?"

It is vital that you allow the other person to respond to your assertion. They may agree with what you have said or they may not. They have a right to disagree with you and, by the same token, you have the right to calmly but assertively repeat your point. It is called the broken record technique precisely because you repeat your request as many times as is necessary.

James used the broken record technique when returning goods.

James: *"I bought this jacket earlier today and, when I got home, found that two buttons are missing and part of the inside lining was ripped. I would like a new jacket or my money back please."*

Sales person: *"We only sell high quality jackets. We don't sell them with missing buttons or torn lining, Sir."*

James: *"I'm sure you don't normally, but this one did have missing buttons and ripped lining. I would like a new jacket or my money back."*

Sales person: *"Some people inadvertently damage their goods and then say they bought them that way."*

James: *"Perhaps some people do. But I didn't. I would like a new jacket or my money back."*

Sales person: *"We don't have any more of that brand in your size. You'll have to keep it."*

James: *"I don't want to keep this jacket because it has missing buttons and ripped lining. I want a new jacket or my money back."*

Sales person: *"I have a lot of other customers to attend to. I can't spend all day discussing this with you."*

James: *"I also don't want to spend all day discussing it with you. As soon as I get a new jacket or my money back I will be on my way."*

Sales person: *"OK, I have new stock coming in first thing tomorrow morning. If you can come back then I can exchange the jacket."*

James: *"Thank you."*

Remember to be polite and to vary the words you use so you don't sound like a Dalek. Eventually the other person will acquiesce and hopefully agree with your request. If necessary, you may need to seek a compromise, enabling the situation to become a win-win as opposed to an *"I win-you lose"* situation.

The fogging technique

We have all been on the receiving end of individuals who believe they have to put us down. No matter how eloquent we may be, dealing with somebody that behaves in an aggressive, bullying or manipulative manner can leave even the most experienced of us lost for words.

Fogging is an assertiveness skill that involves agreeing with any truth that may be contained within a person's statements. The idea was developed by Manuel J Smith in his book *When I Say No, I Feel Guilty*. By not responding in the expected way, in other words, by not being defensive or argumentative, the other person will tend to stop their confrontation as their desired effect will not be achieved. When the atmosphere is less heated, it will be possible to discuss the issues more reasonably.

Fogging is so termed because you act like a wall of fog. No one can hit a fog. You can't dent it; it doesn't care what you do to it, and you can't hurt its feelings. It remains calm until it's ready to go away. Fogging off criticism works in a similar way.

Fogging is a very practical technique and a way to accept criticism without it bringing you down.

If someone says to you:

"That is really poor, sloppy work. The quality has really gone downhill."

You respond by agreeing in the following manner:

"I agree this is not my best work, but with a more realistic timeframe and a realistic budget, I could have done a lot better."

Here are some other examples:

"Do you realise it's 7pm? You're over an hour late and we won't have time to eat before the show starts!"

Response:

"Yes, I am late. I just couldn't get away from work on time. I can see that this has angered you."

The other person might then say:

"Of course I'm angry. I just don't like being kept waiting! I'm also cold and hungry!"

Response:

"I was concerned that I would be keeping you waiting and we would not have time to eat. Perhaps we can eat after the show?"

"So what kept you at work?"

The person accusing you will eventually run out of accusations to throw.

Explain this technique to a friend, someone you trust, and have them insult you non-stop for five minutes while you respond with the fogging technique. It can even be fun to practise.

Negative enquiry

This is a technique you can use to handle the type of criticism that pushes your emotional buttons and makes you feel bad about yourself. It works by asking the other person to clarify the criticism aimed at you. In other words, you ask them what they think you are doing wrong, and what you could do to rectify the situation.

Here are some examples:

Criticism

"You are just so critical of me."

Response

"In what way do you think I'm critical of you?"

Criticism

"You are a really poor tennis player."

Response

"Would you give me some examples of my poor tennis playing?"

The negative enquiry can be a helpful technique because if people are attempting to manipulate you with vague criticisms, they will soon stop when they are unable to respond with specific constructive criticism. If they do come up with a valid criticism, you can view this as feedback that will enable you to change your behaviour in a positive way.

Remember to take your time responding to people. Clarify in your own mind what you want to say before you respond to someone's request.

Don't apologise to people for saying, 'no' as this gives them the message that you're unsure or that your needs are unimportant.

It's good to talk

Communication is one of the most important life skills. We all need to communicate, but although we have been doing so since childhood, many of us lack the necessary skills to communicate effectively. Communication is the act of sending information from one place to another in written, digital or visual form. We also communicate non-verbally, using body language, gestures and the tonality of our voice.

Effective communication is about more than just exchanging information; it's about understanding the emotion behind that information. Good communication skills are the key to developing friendships and building strong and lasting relationships. They help take care of our own needs, while being respectful of the needs of others. People aren't born with good communication skills; like any other skill, they are learned through trial, error and repeated practice.

By deepening our connections to others and improving our decision-making and problem-solving skills, we are better able to communicate even negative or difficult messages without experiencing conflict or destroying trust. Good communication incorporates a set of skills including non-verbal communication, attentive and active listening, the ability to manage stress in the moment, and the capacity to recognise and understand our emotions and those of the person we are communicating with.

Effective communication occurs only when the listener clearly understands the message that you, the speaker, intended to send. By developing our communication skills, we can improve our professional, social and personal relationships. Indeed, many areas of our life can be enriched by expanding and sharpening these skills.

Rethink it!
Essential communication skills
1. Active listening

You may be surprised to learn that listening is an important skill within the communication process. How well you listen has a major impact on your effectiveness as a communicator and on the quality of your relationships with others. Listening enables a person to obtain accurate information, understand the other person, and avoid misunderstandings and conflict.

Active listening involves:

- Looking at the other person directly.
- Not being distracted by other thoughts.
- Not mentally rehearse a rebuttal while the person is talking.
- Using body language to show that you are

listening, such as nodding, smiling and the occasional verbal comment (i.e., 'yes', 'uh-huh', etc.).

- Providing feedback by paraphrasing what the other person is saying. This enables us to understand accurately what she or he means without allowing our own beliefs and judgments to cloud what we hear.

Feedback can consist of the following forms of paraphrasing:

"What I hear you saying is ..."

"It sounds like you mean ..."

You can use these forms of paraphrasing by summarising periodically.

It is important to allow the speaker to finish making his or her point without interrupting with counter arguments. Once the person has finished, it's your turn to respond in an open, honest and respectful way. Remember, effective communication takes place only when the listener clearly understands the message that the speaker intended to send.

2. Verbal communication

We wish to convey our message succinctly and accurately. However, it's all too easy for messages to be misinterpreted. Pitfalls can include talking too much or too little, overcomplicating how we convey our message by using jargon, going off track with our message and failing to bring our subject to life. Vague language can confuse and leave the listener unsure of what message is being conveyed. Emotive words can inflame a conversation and inhibit communication. The result of this could be that the listener carries out an activity that you did not want, or misunderstands and then feels defensive or angry. It is therefore important to think about the message that we wish to deliver.

Think about:

- The objective or purpose of the message
- What you wish to achieve
- How the other person will receive the message
- How you can express the message so that you minimise potential misunderstandings and defensiveness from the other person

Paying attention to the words and phrases you use will help to ensure you aren't misunderstood. Successful communication happens when you are able to make people believe in what you are saying to them. To do this, you need to be sincere and enthusiastic and have all the facts needed to back up the message.

3. Non-verbal communication

Our non-verbal communication is just as important as verbal communication, and includes our body movement, the tonality of our voice, and the space and territory that we occupy. Our non-verbal communication can convey to others how interested or disinterested we are in them, and whether we agree or disagree with what they have to say. Poor body language can significantly contribute to the breakdown of good communication.

To enhance your non-verbal communication, pay attention to:

A. Body movements

Be aware of the messages you are giving to others through your body movement. Nodding, sincere facial expressions and good eye contact will all convey interest to the other person. Our hands are our most expressive body parts, conveying even more than our faces. In a conversation, moving your hand behind your head usually reflects negative thoughts, feelings and moods. It may be a sign of uncertainty, conflict, disagreement, frustration, anger or dislike. Leaning back and clasping both hands behind the neck is often a sign of dominance. Pay attention to the possibility of mismatched expressions. An example of a mismatched expression would be smiling throughout an apology to someone for treating him or her badly.

It is also important to be aware of other people's body language as it can offer important feedback. For instance, if the other person's body language seems to suggest that she or he is not happy with what you are saying, you could ask what it is that's causing concern. Individuals from different cultures may assign very different meanings to facial expressions, use of space and, especially, gestures. For example, in some Asian cultures, women learn that it is disrespectful to look people in the eye and so they tend to have downcast eyes during a conversation. But in the West, this body language could be misinterpreted as disinterestedness or a lack of attention.

B. Pay attention to how your voice sounds. Be mindful of raising your voice in an angry tone. Remember that it's not necessarily what is being said, but how it is said. A simple request can be taken completely the wrong way if said in a raised or unintentionally threatening tone.

C. Space and territorial boundaries

We've all experienced violations to our personal space, whether it is an awkward situation in which someone is standing too close to you, is yelling across the room, or has just taken your favourite seat at the cinema. In order to communicate effectively, we need to be aware of our space as well as the space of others. You may have seen the popular comedy sketches where two people start in one area of the room and one person moves closer, while the other moves further away. This goes on until eventually one person is up against a wall with nowhere to go.

Be aware of how others feel about their space. By consciously and actively being aware of our body language, we can defuse the potential for misunderstandings in our interactions. Effective communication can be challenging. However, by developing your skills through practice, you can become a good communicator.

Relationship matters

Relationships are an essential aspect of people's lives. When our relationships are going well, we can feel on top of the world. We are happy, inspired and energetic. When our relationships are problematic, our world seems to be filled with feelings of sadness and doubt.

Most people experience issues with their partners. Financial concerns, bringing up children, and sexual and emotional problems, including infidelity, can put immense pressure on relationships and family life. This can sometimes lead to depression and anxiety in either partner. Every couple is made up of two distinctly different people, with different experiences, interests and emotional needs. Regardless of the compatibility a couple creates in their relationship, they will at times have different perspectives on issues and those differences can lead to conflict. In this segment, I am going to give you some practical ideas and tips, including a plan of action that can help you get your intimate relationship back on track, and turn a relatively trouble-free relationship into an even better one.

Acknowledge a problem exists

It is not unusual for one partner to believe that there is a problem within their relationship while the other partner cannot or will not see or acknowledge that a problem exists. People sometimes dismiss their partner's concerns out of hand, telling them they are worrying about nothing, perhaps nagging or even being paranoid. However, if one partner perceives there to be a problem within the relationship then, by definition, a problem exists and will need to be addressed and resolved by both partners. If both partners acknowledge there is a problem then an important step has already been taken towards resolving it, allowing both to reconnect and strengthen their relationship.

Rethink it!

TIP: Listen

The fact that relationships change over time is natural and inevitable. What you wanted from a relationship in the early stages might be very different from what you want after you have been together a number of years. Changes occur in other areas of our life, such as at work, and will have an impact on what someone wants and needs from their relationship. It is important that each partner listens attentively to what the other wants. A lot of careful, clear communication has to take place. Change can be stressful, yet due to its inevitability, welcoming rather than resisting change will give a couple an opportunity to enhance their relationship. Planning for changes together can reduce stress and enable a relationship to grow.

Stop the blame game

If you're experiencing conflict with your partner, it's likely you feel overwhelmed with emotion at times, and find it hard to think clearly. Sometimes anger gets the better of us. We might say things that we later wish we had not said. Couples often get stuck in a negative and unending pattern of argument about relationship difficulties. This destructive behaviour can become a regular occurrence and spiral out of control. When it comes to placing blame in a relationship, it's almost always easier to see the fault in the other person rather than in ourselves. For instance, one partner can feel overwhelmingly convinced that they are the completely innocent party and tell themselves that they have every right to blame their partner. When a discussion is not working and spirals into a destructive argument, the most effective thing to do for the welfare of both partners and the relationship is to call time out. Picking at a scab repeatedly will not help the scab to heal.

TIP: Timeout

When you're in the heat of an argument, it can be difficult to think clearly; it is as if the couple is in a 'fight or flight' state of mind. This means that they are seeing each other as either a predator or prey. Listening to one another becomes almost impossible in such situations. There's only a feeling of being defensive, going into withdrawal, attacking or running away. Taking a timeout can help both of you to calm down, giving your emotions a chance to settle. Do not leave the situation without providing an explanation, and agree to discuss the issue at a later time.

Together, decide on a stop phrase such as

'timeout'. Then, when an argument is building up and one of you believes it is becoming destructive, you or your partner uses the agreed upon phrase – for example: *"I am taking timeout and will be back in an hour."* The person that makes the statement should then leave the room. Note that these words include an important message about when the person will be back. By stating this, it minimises the chances that your partner will think you are running away from the problem.

If your partner calls a timeout, you must let him or her leave the room without questioning the decision or piling on more blame. After all, you made an agreement with your partner that you would stop talking and let him or her leave the room. Taking timeouts can go a long way towards restoring trust in a relationship that has been damaged by destructive arguments and behaviour.

Focus on solutions and a plan of action

Relationships are an area of our lives where effective planning may be regarded as too clinical and unnecessary. The idea that couples should create a plan in order to meet each other's most important emotional and practical needs seems to go against relationship intuition.

Couples may believe that they should be guided by their instincts whenever they have a conflict or if something practical needs to be addressed. However, in order to resolve relationship problems it can be beneficial to create an effective plan of action.

Create and implement a plan that will resolve your conflicts and bring you closer together by:

A: Listing the issues

Write down the issues that you both argue about and which you believe are damaging your relationship. This needs to include those issues you have been too fearful to talk about. Your list needs to be phrased positively, without criticism, complaints, blame, accusations, anger or sarcasm.

B: Being specific

It is vital that you and your partner create a list that is specific and realistic. If it's too vague, it won't be concrete enough, and if it's too long, you may not know where to start. If your list seems endless and you cannot agree on what to include, you may need to look at your communication style first and possibly seek the help of a relationship therapist.

C: Brainstorming for practical, realistic solutions

Your goal is to find mutually agreeable solutions to all of the issues; in the process of achieving this, you'll learn new skills that will help you to resolve other issues as they arise. Each person needs to think of concrete, realistic and practical things they can do to improve the situation. For example, if you never seem to get enough time together, your aim will be to optimise your schedules to make time for each other. You may write down something like:

Make time for a cup of tea together before we start our

day.

Spend at least 30 minutes together before turning in to briefly go over each other's day.

Do one fun thing together at the weekend.

However, if you have young children, your plan may include:

We will ask our respective parents, a close friend, godparent or qualified childminder if they will watch the kids one evening a week.

It is vital that you are patient and give your plan time to work. Review your plan with your partner on a weekly basis, and discuss how well you both believe it is working. If necessary, you can revise the plan together.

REMEMBER

Positive and happy relationships don't happen; they take work. Successful relationships occur when couples risk sharing what's going on in their heads and hearts. If you want changes you need to communicate so your partner knows what you need.

Demonstrate your love for your partner every day. You have the opportunity to make your relationship deeper and more enduring by recommitting to your loved one. Feeling honoured and cherished by the one you love makes life rich and meaningful.

Anger is a self-defeating and destructive emotion. It damages relationships because it keeps you focused on the bad and blinds you to all that is good within your partnership. If you are angry with your partner, take a timeout to calm down and then focus on what's going on for you.

Is your partner also your best friend? This may sound unromantic, but ask any long-term happily married couple and most will tell you that friendship is one of the most important ingredients of their relationship.

You and only you are responsible for your own happiness. Nobody else can make you happy. Unfortunately, one of the biggest relationship mistakes also happens to be one of the most seductive things to do within a partnership − that is to make your partner responsible for your happiness and blame him or her when you are not happy.

If you feel it's your partner's fault, think again. Don't expect one person to meet all your needs. Instead take responsibility for your own happiness. By doing so, you open the door to a relationship based on honesty, integrity and responsibility.

Overcoming Blushing

Have you ever believed yourself to be the centre of attention and that everyone is looking at you? Perhaps someone has singled you out, putting you on the spot by asking you a question in front of a group of people. Maybe in a work meeting your boss surprised you by asking a question that you could not answer or someone cracked a joke that you found sexist or embarrassing. Being put on the spot is a primary trigger for blushing as it involves situations that you weren't expecting to happen. You blush, feel embarrassed and worry that others may see your red face and judge you negatively. Indeed for some people, the fear of blushing can be so intense that they literally bring the blushing on themselves even in relatively stress free situations.

Blushing is Natural

To blush is a perfectly natural function. It is nature's way of revealing our true feelings – an instantaneous physiological response to situations we find embarrassing or anxiety provoking. However some people suffer from more frequent or intense blushing. This can become physically and psychologically tormenting, especially when it occurs as a response to minor prompts or for no apparent reason. People who blush frequently often report that they go bright red when they least expect to, such as when running into a friend on the street, being introduced to somebody new or, even, when paying for an item in a shop. Blushing can be less of an issue when it occurs in what is considered to be more appropriate social situations, such as when receiving public recognition or having *Happy Birthday* sung to them in a restaurant. Each person has his or her own trigger for blushing. However, turning red for no apparent reason causes much distress. Our perception of a situation, and a fear of a negative evaluation by others, creates unhelpful emotions literally brining on the blushing we are so desperate to avoid in the first place.

Sally's checkout nightmare

Sally is a chronic blusher. She believes that practically any interaction involving people she doesn't know well and, some she does know, will make her blush.

"I've started to blush every time I get to the cashier at my checkout in the supermarket. I just cannot help it. As I queue, I'm telling myself 'I mustn't blush.' But I just know I will. I have even started to use the auto checkouts. However the other day, I went to get in line at one and someone said I had jumped the queue. They were very polite about it and it was a tiny misunderstanding but I felt like my face could keep an auditorium warm such was the intensity of my facial flush. One of the most common things I hear said to me is 'Ooh, you've gone bright red.' As if I didn't know! When people tell me I am blushing I feel they are judging me negatively which just makes my blushing worse."

Jim hates being recognized.

"I'm a chronic blusher and I hate it. I blush if I have to give presentations at work and I blush if someone calls out my name in a crowded room. Only the other day at a conference my manager walked into the room, which was very crowded, and at the top of his voice called out 'Jim is July's top salesman.' Despite the fact that it was a complement I went bright red. Then someone said 'Jim, are you embarrassed?' And I flushed even more. My blushing

seems to occur when I least want to be noticed and it can draw attention and some unpleasant comments from people who think they are being funny."

Anxiety about blushing

Anxiety about blushing is often associated with a social anxiety disorder. Many people who seek help for blushing meet the criteria for a social phobia or anxiety. However not everyone who blushes has social anxiety, and not every person with social anxiety blushes. It is the worry and fear about blushing that sets up the conditions that cause us to blush so frequently. This, coupled with the anxiety about how we think others will view us, makes us believe that blushing is a dreadful thing for us to do. These fears frequently lead to low self-worth, lack of confidence, and feelings of helplessness.

You can read more about social anxiety in part two, under the section *Anxiety*.

Rethink it!

Five steps to overcoming blushing

1 Relax your blushing away.

When we blush we can become tense and embarrassed. The more we demand we not blush the more we do blush. This leads to a vicious circle of anxiety, tension and embarrassment and more blood is forced to the face. There are many forms of relaxation that can help you relax your blushing away. Here are two:

A brief relaxation technique if you feel your blushing coming on:

- Begin by becoming aware of where you are holding tension in your body and know you must relax that tension away.
- Drop your shoulders.
- Take slow comfortable deep breaths in through your nose and out though your mouth.
- Repeat a word to yourself such as *'calm'* or *'relax.'*

A longer relaxation technique that involves breathing slowly and deeply. Practice on a regular basis especially before an event that might lead you to blush:

- Sit down in a comfortable place.
- Tune into the rhythm of your breathing.
- Put your hand on your stomach.
- As you breathe, try to feel your stomach moving up and down. The aim is to breathe from your stomach instead of from your chest.
- Slow down the rate of your breathing.

At first, you may find it difficult to breathe from your stomach. To get a comfortable rhythm you may find it helpful to say the word *'re-la-x'* as you breathe out. As you keep practicing, you will find your body becoming more relaxed

Relaxation helps to train your body to let go whenever

you feel the blushing coming on, or feel that you might go red.

2 Acceptance

It is difficult to accept the fact that you are a blusher. However that is precisely what you need to do. Do not try to fight it. This will only make your blushing worse. When you think you are going to blush, it is a natural response to try and fight it, but as I am sure you have already discovered, this just increases your anxiety levels. It is this heightened anxiety, particularly in social situations, that causes you to blush. You need to change your attitude towards your blushing. At the moment you may hold a belief such as:

"I absolutely must not blush and if I do it's terrible. People will judge me harshly."

Instead try telling yourself:

"At the moment, I am a blusher. It's just what my body does. I don't like it but I can handle it and still accept myself in spite of my blushing."

Try to adopt a, *"so what, it's not the end of the world"* attitude towards your blushing.

If you can learn to accept yourself in spite of the fact that you blush you will start to take the pressure off yourself and the blushing is far more likely to go away.

Try not to define yourself by your blushing. Give it an insignificant place in your life. You could ask yourself, *"What would I do if I didn't have this blushing issue?"* Then, consider whether you can do these things in spite of the blushing. Value yourself regardless of the blushing. This may not be easy; but it's not impossible and certainly worth the effort.

You will find more about how to stop blushing in Part One, *What do you say when you talk to yourself.*

3 Fear of being judged

We blush when we are embarrassed, and then become embarrassed because we are blushing. We then blush even more. Much of the embarrassment about blushing is caused by the belief that others will judge us harshly. We may believe that they will think that we are weak and naive. This type of distortion in our thinking is referred to as mind reading and occurs when we make an assumption that other people are looking down on us, and where we become so convinced about this that we don't even bother to check it out.

You can challenge your mind reading by asking yourself the following:

"What is the evidence that I am being judged?"

"How do I know what other people are thinking?"

"Just because I assume something, does that mean I'm right?"

"If someone is thinking negatively about me, does that mean I have to agree with them?"

Everyone has had the unfortunate experience of being embarrassed and most decent people will be sympathetic about it. If people are thinking what you think they are thinking, does this mean something negative about you – such as you are weak or stupid? Or does it say more about them, such as they're judgmental and just plain wrong! Anyone who thinks less of you for blushing is most probably not worth knowing.

4 Announce your blushing

One thing that can keep your blushing well and truly active is the attempt to hide it. Pretending that it's not happening keeps blushing alive and will mean that you blush more often. You try to hide it because you perceive it as embarrassing. However many people have found it helpful to announce they are blushing as it is about to happen. This might appear to be a counterproductive or even crazy idea. However by making light of your blushing, you learn to accept it and remove some of the heat, as well as relieve the pressure on yourself.

Examples of announcing your blushing include:

"Here I go, I'm about to go red."

"I think I might blush."

This in turn can diminish the frequency of your blushing.

5 Invite the symptoms

Many of my clients find that the more they try and stop blushing the more they blush. It seems to be a vicious cycle. Some of my clients have been helped by a technique called *The Paradoxical approach:*

Peter was a regular blusher. He would blush when he

was first introduced to people at work or socially. He would even blush when going into a newsagent to purchase a paper.

Peter had tried many techniques to stop blushing such as relaxation and telling himself it didn't really matter if he blushed – all to no avail. Nothing seemed to help Peter.

I suggested to Peter that he *'invite the symptom.'*

I gave him the homework assignment of deliberately trying to blush for 6 minutes 3 times a day every day for a week. I asked Peter to keep a diary of the blushing sessions and the degree to which he was able to make himself blush. He could start at home then progress to trying to make himself blush when in public. He was also to keep note of the times he blushed when he wasn't deliberately trying to make it happen.

At first Peter resisted the idea thinking it nonsense. But gradually he started to practice deliberately making himself blush. Peter discovered that he had far more control over his blushing than he believed and that he could cope with the uncertainty of blushing itself. Gradually his non-deliberate blushing started to decrease as he accepted that he could cope. He had diminished the power blushing had over him.

Once we learn to stop struggling and trying to force the blushing away then we can start to reduce it. This requires work and practice, with a willingness to be kind and accept yourself. With patience you can do it.

Blushing can be a symptom of a medical complaint, always seek medical advice just to be safe.

About the author

Michael Cohen is a Cognitive Behavioural Hypnotherapist and Psychotherapist with 28 years of clinical experience. He runs a busy practice in London and is a specialist in the treatment of anxiety disorders, which includes stress, anxiety, panic attacks, panic disorders, lack of confidence, phobias, social anxiety, health anxiety and much more.

Michael has made many radio and television appearances and is featured often in the national press. He is the author of *Identifying Understanding and Solutions to Stress* as well as the No 1 selling self-help book *The Power of Accepting Yourself*.

RECOMMENDED READING

For the Challenges of Life
The Power of Accepting Yourself
Michael Cohen. Bookline & Thinker Ltd

How to Cope When the Going Gets Tough
Dr Windy Dryden and Jack Gordon. Sheldon Press

For Emotional Misery and Depression
The Feeling Good Handbook
David Burns MD. Penguin Books Ltd

Overcoming Depression
Dr Paul Gilbert. Constable and Robinson

For Anxiety and Fear
Master Your Panic and Take Back Your Life
Denise F Beckfield PH.D. Impact

*When Panic Attacks: The New Drug-Free Anxiety Therapy
That Can Change Your Life*
David Burns. Vermillion

For Confidence and Self-Acceptance
Hold Your Head Up

Paul Hauck. Sheldon Press

Building Self-Confidence for Dummies
Kate Burton. John Wiley & Sons

Relationships and Assertiveness
Your Perfect Right
Robert Alberti PH.D and Michael Emmons PH.D. Impact

The Relate Guide to Better Relationships: Practical Ways to Make Your Love Last From the Experts in Marriage Guidance Relate Guides
Sarah Litvinoff. Vermillion

Useful websites

If you would like to know more about Cognitive Behaviour Therapy and Clinical Hypnotherapy then the following websites may be of use:

In The UK
Michael Cohen (author and therapist)
www.hypnosisandhealing.co.uk

British Association for Behavioural and Cognitive Psychotherapies
www.babcp.com

The Association for Rational Emotive Behaviour Therapy
http://www.arebt.eu

National Council for Hypnotherapy.
www.hypnotherapists.org.uk

In the USA
Beck Institute for Cognitive Therapy and Research
www.beckinstitute.org

The Albert Ellis Institute
www.rebt.org

National Guild of Hypnotists
www.ngh.net

Acknowledgements

With thanks to Marianne Makdisi and Lisa Lee for their help.